Museum Operations

ABOUT THE SERIES

The American Association for State and Local History Book Series addresses issues critical to the field of state and local history through interpretive, intellectual, scholarly, and educational texts. To submit a proposal or manuscript to the series, please request proposal guidelines from AASLH headquarters: AASLH Editorial Board, 1717 Church St., Nashville, Tennessee 37203. Telephone: (615) 320-3203. Website: www.aaslh.org.

ABOUT THE ORGANIZATION

The American Association for State and Local History (AASLH) is a national history membership association headquartered in Nashville, Tennessee. AASLH provides leadership and support for its members who preserve and interpret state and local history in order to make the past more meaningful to all Americans. AASLH members are leaders in preserving, researching, and interpreting traces of the American past to connect the people, thoughts, and events of yesterday with the creative memories and abiding concerns of people, communities, and our nation today. In addition to sponsorship of this book series, AASLH publishes *History News* magazine, a newsletter, technical leaflets and reports, and other materials; confers prizes and awards in recognition of outstanding achievement in the field; supports a broad education program and other activities designed to help members work more effectively; and advocates on behalf of the discipline of history. To join AASLH, go to www.aaslh.org or contact Membership Services, AASLH, 1717 Church St., Nashville, TN 37203.

Museum Operations

A Handbook of Tools, Templates, and Models

Samantha Chmelik

ROWMAN & LITTLEFIELD
Lanham • Boulder • New York • London

Published by Rowman & Littlefield
A wholly owned subsidary of The Rowman & Littlefield Publishing Group, Inc.
4501 Forbes Boulevard, Suite 200, Lanham, Maryland 20706
www.rowman.com

Unit A, Whitacre Mews, 26-34 Stannary Street, London SE11 4AB

British Library Cataloguing in Publication Information Available

Library of Congress Cataloging-in-Publication Data

Names: Chmelik, Samantha, 1971- author.
Title: Museum operations : a handbook of tools, templates, and models /
    Samantha Chmelik.
Description: Lanham : Rowman & Littlefield, 2017. | Series: American
    Association for State and Local History book series | Includes
    bibliographical references and index.
Identifiers: LCCN 2016050185 (print) | LCCN 2016052426 (ebook) | ISBN
    9781442270473 (cloth) | ISBN 9781442270480 (pbk.) | ISBN 9781442270497
    (ebook)
Subjects: LCSH: Museums—Research—Methodology. |
    Museums—Management—Research—Methodology. |
    Museums—Planning—Research—Methodology. | Museums—Research—Case
    studies. | Museums—Management—Research—Case studies. |
    Museums—Planning—Research—Case studies.
Classification: LCC AM5 .C47 2017 (print) | LCC AM5 (ebook) | DDC 069—dc23
    LC record available at https://lccn.loc.gov/2016050185

Printed in the United States of America

To the volunteers, staff, and board members
at museums, historic sites, and nonprofit organizations

Contents

List of Figures and Tables

LIST OF FIGURES

LIST OF TABLES

Preface

Computers, software, and other technologies facilitate our ability to conduct the business of museums more efficiently and effectively. Financial projections, label publishing, graphic design, and myriad other tasks have been streamlined and simplified due to technology. The fundamental processes and procedures that we use to manage these different types of projects, to conduct research, to analyze information, and to craft recommendations or strategic plans remain the same—even if we use a computer program to guide the process and capture the results. Understanding the basics of project management and using tools, templates, and models allow us to maximize our resources and time in environments where both are constrained. The less time spent on administrative or pure process aspects of a project, the more time can be spent on the research, analysis, and recommendations that will help your institution.

Throughout our careers, almost daily, we are asked to research, analyze, and recommend products, services, policies, methodologies, procedures, tactics, and strategies. As we move from straightforward questions (e.g., "which blog platform will work best for our institution?") to more complex questions (e.g., "what is our five-year strategic plan?"), we need a structured, manageable way to gather data, review and analyze findings, and craft recommendations. *Museum Operations: A Handbook of Tools, Templates, and Models* provides the structures, procedures, tools, templates, and models that can be used to conduct research projects, analyze results, develop recommendations, and then present those results to fellow museum professionals, board members, and other institutional stakeholders.

With the myriad data and research sources available, organizing and analyzing that information can be difficult. If you don't focus your efforts, the research and recommendation process is nearly impossible, frustrating, and exhausting. This book lays a practical foundation by presenting the tools, templates, and models business professionals use to plan and execute research projects, analyze data, craft recommendations, and present their results.

Using these tools, templates, and models has three benefits. First, your board members, funders, and supporters whose experience is primarily in the for-profit arena will be familiar with many of them and may feel more comfortable discussing tactics and strategies using these items as touchstones. Second, using these tools, templates, and models shows the logic or thought process you used to develop your recommendations—providing a deeper level of understanding for people who may be reading the document at a later date. Third, using them also allows you easily to update or replicate your research and analyses. If a circumstance or data point changes, you can return to the original document, revise the relevant information, and then update your analyses. If your document contains only conclusions or recommendations, you may not know how different variables or data points impact one another. The transparency and easy replication of these tools, templates, and models facilitates future updates.

This book is organized into four parts. Each part can be read independently or nonconsecutively, depending on your needs or familiarity with the subjects. The four parts are:

- Part I—The Research Project Tutorial
- Part II—Tools, Templates, and Models Instructions
- Part III—Case Studies
- Part IV—Tools, Templates, and Models Worksheets

Part I—The Research Project Tutorial is a step-by-step guide to conducting a research project. The research process presented here provides you with the essential elements of designing and implementing a research project. You will learn how to write a research question, plan a project, select data sources, and present research results. Experienced researchers or project managers may prefer to skim or skip part I.

This book follows the general theories of project management as developed by the Project Management Institute and is based on my project management experience. For those interested in a more rigorous approach, the Project Management Institute offers classes and certifications. Industry associations (e.g., the American Association for State and Local History and universities also offer project management classes), apps, and collaborative software (e.g., Trello or Basecamp) also follow project management tenets. The Resource List at the end of the book contains additional sources of project management software and training, as well as other reporting and visualization software. (Free or low-cost versions of all of the listed software are available.) Select the software or app or training that is most relevant for you.

Part II—Tools, Templates, and Models Instructions introduces nineteen tools, templates, and models. You will learn how and when to use each one, as well as their individual advantages and drawbacks. You will also see how using them can save you time and money by helping you efficiently and effectively use your resources. Sample versions with examples are presented.

The tools are:

- Search Planning Worksheet
- Vendor Questionnaire
- Project Budget Worksheet
- Project Charter
- Tree Diagram
- Cause and Effect Diagram
- Flowchart
- Force Field Analysis
- Matrix Diagram
- Blind-Spot Worksheet

The templates are:

- SWOT—Strengths, Weaknesses, Opportunities, Threats
- Swim Lanes
- Matrix-Gantt Chart
- Executive Summary Report
- Managerial Report

The models are:

- GAP Model: Services
- Risk Mitigation Model
- PESTLE—Political, Economic, Social, Technological, Legal, and Ecological
- Scenario Planning Matrix

You may already be familiar with some of these items; others may be new. You may be using some of these tools, templates, and models without knowing their formal names or structures. You may use some of them frequently and never use others. You may also find that board members or other stakeholders prefer certain tools, templates, and models and don't use others. Your needs and preferences will determine your usage.

Tools, templates, and models can be used on their own or in conjunction with one another. Part II also shows how different ones complement others. Sometimes they can be selected at the outset of a project. In other cases, they may be incorporated as a project evolves. Understanding the purpose of each tool, template, and model allows you to select the most appropriate item when needed.

Part III—Case Studies presents six fictional case studies of how museums of any budget or staff size can use these tools, templates, and models to facilitate research, decision making, and strategic planning. Their use or order of use in these case studies should not be viewed as the only or the definitive way to incorporate tools, templates, or models into the research or decision-making process. As you read the case studies, you may want to consider how the use of a different tool, template, or model might affect the protagonists' assessment of their situations and their final decisions. You may choose to read part III before parts I or II to visualize more effectively when and how you might use them in your institution.

The most important lesson from part III is the use of different tools, templates, and models to introduce and guide discussions of difficult or controversial issues constructively. Several are constructed to capture multiple points of view and to assess their likelihood or impact. Participants can then see that their input has been recorded and evaluated in a fair and productive manner.

Part IV—Tools, Templates, and Models Worksheets contains the blank worksheet versions of the nineteen tools, templates, and models that you can use in your work. Each worksheet has instructions and a recommended completion time to guide your use. All of them originally were created to improve our efficiency and to reduce the time spent on these activities. The focus always should be on achieving your goals and objectives, not exhaustively completing these worksheets.

Depending on your issue, team size, or other circumstance, you may need to adapt these versions for your project. Typically you might add or subtract topics, personnel involved, or time lines. The four models and the Blind-Spot Worksheet are the only items whose fundamental structure cannot be changed or adapted or customized.

As shown in the case studies, several of these tools, templates, and models can be used in the same project, or your project may consist of completing one model or worksheet as a group exercise. All of them were selected for inclusion because of their flexibility, scalability, and applicability in institutions of any staff or budget size. As you use these tools, templates, and models, you will become more comfortable with adaptations.

This book is designed to demystify the research, project management, and decision-making processes by supplying the tools, templates, and models to conduct, manage, and analyze research effectively and efficiently. Using them will help you:

- save time and expenses
- maximize the use of search engines and other research resources

- use the most appropriate analytical models
- integrate research results and institutional strategy and objectives
- craft well-designed, engaging reports and presentations

Project management helps us use our time wisely; research enlightens us; analyzing information broadens our perspective; decisions explicate the goals and objectives used in fulfilling our institutional mission. You, your board, or other stakeholders will find other useful tools, templates, and models: scraps of paper, an e-mail, a formal worksheet, or computer program all are formats that can be used to manage projects or complete any of the tools, templates, and models in this book. First, you must understand the basics of project management, conducting research, analyzing information, and making decisions before selecting a tool, template, or model, as well as enabling technologies.

Acknowledgments

This book is the amalgamation of projects and writings executed for my research company. I never would have founded that company or explored new career paths without the encouragement and support of Leonard Fuld, a pioneer in competitor research and analysis. My editor, Charles Harmon, patiently waded through myriad tables and charts with encouragement and enthusiasm, which I greatly appreciate.

I hope this handbook helps museum professionals resolve situations effectively and efficiently, as well as facilitates communications with the for-profit professionals whose support and dedication are integral to the success of museums and historic sites.

THE RESEARCH PROJECT TUTORIAL

Before learning about tools, templates, and models, we should first review the context for using them, as well as the project management process. Projects can range from one person searching the Internet to multi-person teams conducting primary and secondary research and then analyzing the results. One e-mail or a software suite may help you manage your project and your team. The basic process of scoping and managing a project is the same regardless of project size or complexity. You select tools and templates to collect and organize your data, then analyze your data and craft your recommendations. You choose templates and models to present your findings and recommendations to others.

Part I breaks down the overall research process into three chapters:

- Chapter 1: Scoping and Managing the Research Project
- Chapter 2: Identifying and Using Data Sources
- Chapter 3: Analyzing and Reporting Research Results

Each chapter delves into the nuts and bolts of these topics. If you have used project management software or taken project management classes, you already should be familiar with these topics. Although individual systems may use slightly different terminology or processes, the general methodology seems familiar, so you may choose to skim or skip part I.

As previously discussed, the complexity of your project will guide your methodology and tool selection. Chapters 1 through 3 provide the broadest context for research project management. The level of detail may seem daunting. You can then adapt, abridge, or eliminate steps that are not germane to your project. You also may not need to write down all of your choices, either. As you become more experienced, you will be able to think through the processes quickly and focus on the research and analyses instead of the mechanics of project management. Understanding the research project process in its entirety will help you decide which tools, methodologies, and processes are most helpful in any circumstance.

CHAPTER 1

SCOPING AND MANAGING THE RESEARCH PROJECT

Museums conduct a variety of research projects, ranging from visitor surveys to vendor evaluations to funding sources. For example, your institution may participate in the American Association of State and Local History's Visitors Count! program to better understand your visitors. Museums may also benchmark themselves against other museums or nonprofit institutions. Reviewing other organizations' 990 forms shows you how other institutions generate income, pay upper-level staff, and allocate resources. Both the 990 analyses and the Visitors Count! program are research projects. The 990 analyses may be conducted by one person over the course of an afternoon, whereas the Visitors Count! program is a multi-person, multi-month research project. No matter the time line or staff involvement, every project begins with a question to be answered. Identifying the core question you need to answer will help you select the appropriate methodologies, tools, techniques, and analytical models to achieve your goal.

To begin, write, as simply as possible, the question(s) you need to answer. Here are some sample questions:

- Is museum visitation in my region shrinking, stable, or growing?
- How does my museum's visitation compare to other local/regional cultural institutions?
- Which other cultural institutions are popular with my visitors? Why?
- How far will people travel to visit my institution?
- Why do people visit my institution?
- What macro changes (e.g., recession/economic boom, population changes, societal trends, technology trends) are affecting my institution? How are they affecting my institution?
- How will pending legislation affect my institution?
- What machines/tools/software/services should my institution use for admissions/membership/the café/the museum store?
- Should I outsource the management of my institution's café/museum store?

Different contexts may drive the same questions. If your visitation is increasing or decreasing, benchmarking your visitation against other institutions will help you determine if the change in visitation is a short-term or long-term trend that requires additional planning. That context will guide the selection of data sources and analytical models that will be discussed later in this book.

RESEARCH PROJECT COMPONENTS

Regardless of project size or complexity, research projects have six main components. For small, one-person projects, a few sentences should describe how you will execute each component. For large, multi-person projects, use the Project Charter tool that will be introduced in part II to ensure that everyone understands his responsibilities. At most, you should need only one to ten pages to explain how you will execute the following six project components:

- Scope and Objectives
- Methodology
- Personnel
- Budget
- Schedule
- Results Analysis and Reporting

If you define each of these areas before beginning a project, your chances of completing the project successfully will improve.

Scope and Objectives

The project scope defines the purpose of your research and should be aligned to a specific management issue. It explains and defines why the research is needed and what the research will accomplish. Writing the scope is analogous to writing the thesis paragraph of a term paper. At this stage, you are defining the purpose and objectives of your research—not advancing any theories or predictions about the research results or subsequent analysis. After establishing the scope, you outline your objectives, which will generate your research questions. Ultimately, answering those research questions will provide the information you need to complete your objectives and fulfill your scope.

For example, multiple key staff members have left the fictional Welltech Science Museum for other institutions. In their exit interviews, all of the departing staff stated that Welltech's salaries and benefits were significant factors in their exits. So the museum director tasks the human resources director with benchmarking Welltech's salaries and benefits against similar institutions and proposing any adjustments that should be made.

The project scope is to benchmark Welltech's salaries and benefits against those offered at other science museums, nationally and locally. The objectives within that scope include:

- identifying all possible staff benefits
- matching Welltech job descriptions with standard museum job descriptions
- comparing Welltech salaries against salaries at similar institutions
- determining any changes to Welltech's compensation package

Each objective generates a corresponding research question (e.g., what are the different benefits offered to museum staff?). As you can see, some of these questions are answered with data, whereas others are answered by analyzing the data collected during the research phase.

As the project progresses, you may learn that the original objectives are incomplete or not applicable to the scope. At that point, the project must be reassessed. You can decide to cancel the project, continue the project as is, or create a new/follow-up project. Avoid the temptation to continue the same project and just expand the scope. "Scope creep" (as this phenomenon is called) typically leads to confusion, extra expense, and inconclusive results. If the original scope and objectives prove unwieldy or impossible to answer in their current form, canceling the project and beginning anew may be the most effective solution.

When you are writing your scope and objectives, another consideration is the final report, also known as the deliverable. Questions to ask include:

- To whom am I presenting this report?
- How will the information be used?
- How will this report be stored or saved when it is finished?

After you have answered those questions, the general structure and format of the final report should become clear. Chapter 3 discusses reporting options in more detail. After establishing the scope and objectives, the next step is to select the research methodology.

Methodology

Methodology explains in a few sentences how you will conduct the research (e.g., a survey or a literature review). Questions to answer include:

- Will we use human sources or published sources?
- What resources do we have readily available?
- What resources will we need to purchase?
- Will we conduct any, part, or all of the research in-house?

Establishing the methodology also helps determine the time frame for the project. A project that requires multiple focus group interviews will take longer than a project based on published source/literature research. If you need to purchase additional resources or distribute Requests for Proposals (RFPs), you have to account for this time as well. After determining which resources you already have, then investigate which need to be purchased and the members of the project team who know how to use the resource(s).

Human Source Research Strategies

Interviewing people may seem daunting, but people usually are willing to share their thoughts if they have time and/or are approached correctly. Have a list of questions ready before calling or walking up to someone. You don't want to waste time trying to find your questions. And don't simply read the list. Few people are enthusiastic about saying yes or no or giving one- or two-word answers for more than a few seconds. Use a question to kick off the interview and ask people to clarify any comments to ensure that you are reporting the meaning accurately. Try to have a conversation with the person, rather than an interrogation. A conversation may elicit previously unknown information or points of view.

Questions come in two main categories: open and closed. Open questions lead to open answers. People answer however they want, like answering an essay question. Examples of open questions include:

- Why did you come to the museum today?
- What was your favorite exhibit?
- How did you compare the job offers you received?
- Why did you choose audio guide vendor A?

Open questions are useful when trying to identify attitudes and behaviors.

Closed questions predetermine the person's options for an answer. Examples of closed questions include: yes/no, true/false, multiple choice, or "rate this on a scale of 1 to 10." Closed questions generate quantifiable answers that can be analyzed statistically. You may need a blend of open and closed questions to collect all of the necessary data. A sandwich technique of beginning with one or two closed questions, moving to the open questions, and ending with the remaining closed questions is effective.

Sharing information is helpful in conversations with experts or colleagues. People are more receptive to talking if they also will learn from the discussion. You need to maintain neutrality in these discussions: your task is to record answers, not to judge them. If the interviewee feels that you prefer or are opposed to some information, she may alter her responses to reduce her or your discomfort. You can ask for additional explanations to ensure that you understand the response, but you should not judge the merit of the response while you are speaking with the person. After you gather your data, you will review its usability and accuracy.

Database Searching: Steps and Strategies

Searching is a practical process that increasingly has been demystified and simplified with the ubiquity of online search tools. Accordingly, organizations choose to conduct their own research, unless specialized expertise or a neutral perspective is necessary. Most people have used Internet search engines (Google) for questions large and small and likely will find aspects of the search process to be familiar. It is essential to outline this practice, however, because search habits are more often poor than good—and good practices are vital to good research and results. The process discussed next will focus on keyword searching and may be used with Internet search engines or commercial databases.

The Search String

Did you know that a specific term describes the words you type into Google? Those words are called a search string. Google and other search engines take those words and translate them into search algorithms, which then determine the results you see. Understanding how Google and other search engines translate the words you type will improve your search results.

Search engines look for the key words. So if you type "what are salaries at science museums?," the search engine translates that question into the phrase "salaries science museum." Then it will look for websites or documents about "salaries," then "science," and finally "museums." The results are ranked according to the amount of content in the Web page or document related to each and all of those concepts. The terminology used and the order of the keywords directly affect the results you see.

Before typing words into a search engine, identify the key concepts of interest and list their synonyms. Then prioritize the concepts of interest. Because the first word is weighted more heavily than the last, type your search string accordingly. In part IV, you will find a Search Planning Worksheet that you can use to plan your search strings. Table 1.1 is an example based on our Welltech Science Museum sample project.

We are looking for salary and benefit information for science museum staff. We need to identify synonyms for "salary and benefits," as well as more specific terms for staff. Consider terms that are broader or narrower than your initial concept. You don't need to be as exhaustive as a thesaurus—just capture the most logical or industry-standard terms to generate the data you need.

Table 1.1. Search Planning Worksheet: Science Museum Staff Salary and Benefits

	Concept 1	**Concept 2**	**Concept 3**
Synonym 1	Salary	Science Museum	Staff
Synonym 2	Benefits	Natural History Museum	Curator
Synonym 3	Compensation	Science Center	Educator
Synonym 4	Wages	Museum	Coordinator
Synonym 5	Remuneration		Programs Manager

Then review your worksheet. For some searches, you may need to account for spelling variations among different languages, regional or national variations of terms (e.g., "substitute teachers" is an American English term, whereas "supply teachers" is the British and Commonwealth English term), or definitional differences between singular and plural versions of a word. Finally, prioritize the synonyms in each concept column. You may decide that the strongest or most relevant search string is "salary curator science museum." Type that search string into your search engine and view the results. If you find the relevant data, then you are done. If you are not satisfied with the results, you have other terms to use. As you review the results, you may uncover additional terms to try.

No "correct" or even best search strategy or search statement exists—only good or poor technique. Understanding how search engines work and completing a Search Planning Worksheet will improve your search technique, efficiency, and results.

Outsourcing Research

For research projects requiring specialized expertise (e.g., focus groups or predictive analyses), or a neutral perspective (e.g., staff reorganization), an outside research vendor may be helpful. You may choose to hire a vendor to supply one very specific service as part of an overall research project or to conduct the entire research project from scope definition to research to analysis and recommendations. Consequently, the cost for their services can range from a few thousand dollars to hundreds of thousands of dollars.

A vendor's expertise could prove invaluable—saving you time and money, as well as providing industry, market, and/or technical expertise. Common sources for locating vendors include:

- conference exhibitors (even if you don't attend, you can see the exhibitor list at the conference website)
- industry association directories
- message boards/discussion forums
- colleagues' recommendations

Before you contact vendors, write a Request for Proposal (RFP). A three- to ten-page RFP will help you organize your thoughts before you contact vendors. First, define the products or services under consideration and then the relevant details for the items, their use, your purchasing process, and your expectations of the vendor. In addition to helping you clarify your thoughts, the RFP helps you compare different vendors effectively. Each vendor will receive the same information about your requirements and should address those requirements in the proposal. You will be able to compare the depth and breadth of those responses quickly. RFPs typically contain:

- a brief description of your institution
- project scope
- the request for a specific service or product (as detailed as possible), including equipment specifications (if applicable), a description of pre-existing internal resources, and a list of services that are not needed (if applicable)
- schedule
- budget range
- personnel who will interact with the vendor (typically the project manager)
- decision-making criteria
- reference request
- contact name
- proposal due date and decision due date

Each of these elements is essential to ensure that the vendor understands your request and that you receive the information needed to evaluate the vendor properly.

After you have written your RFP, you can send it to previously identified vendors and await their proposals. When evaluating the proposals, consider the following criteria:

Industry Experience—How long has the vendor worked in the museum or nonprofit industry? Are they considered experts? Depending on your organization (e.g., art museum or historical society), you may need vendors with subject specialties or with knowledge of the laws/regulations affecting your particular museum type.

General Reputation—What is the "word on the street" about each vendor? What are their strengths and weaknesses? Are they financially stable? Do they have consistent access to the raw materials or staff needed to fulfill your contract? Checking references, Dun & Bradstreet reports, message boards, discussion forums, and news articles will help you answer these questions.

Level of Detail—Does the proposal describe the methodology to be used when conducting the research? What will the deliverable be? Will the deliverable contain actionable recommendations? Are a schedule and budget included? Are terms of payment discussed? What are the project fees, and are costs explained? A good proposal should tell you how, when, and where the work will be conducted and what to expect upon completion.

Customized Proposal—Does the proposal address the issues raised in your RFP? Does it contain references to prior projects that are similar to yours? A good proposal will be a direct response to your RFP, not a standard template sent to anyone who inquires about the vendor's services.

References—Whom may you contact to discuss the work of the vendor? References provide you with the customer perspective about working with the vendor and the usability of the results.

Checking a vendor's reference is a fundamental step that is sometimes skipped. The vendor will give you names of satisfied customers, so why bother calling them? No one is 100 percent satisfied with a vendor; a problem or issue always exists. Even a satisfied customer will have experienced some type of difficulty. The reason a customer is satisfied may be because the vendor resolved the difficulty well. You need that information.

You don't have to rely only on a list of customers from the vendor. Third parties may rate the vendors for a particular product or service. Websites, discussion forums, or message boards could exist where customers discuss and/or rate a particular vendor or a group of vendors. Searching the vendor name and the words "ratings"/"complaints"/"evaluations"/"feedback" may connect you with these user communities. Remember to read these postings with the proverbial grain of salt, especially if the postings are anonymous. If the poster seems objective and rational, then the posting probably is accurate. If the project is a significant financial investment, consider evaluating the financial stability of potential vendors.

Dun & Bradstreet (D&B) is the main source of that financial data. D&B publishes three types of reports about companies: Credit eValuator Plus Report, Business Information Report, and Comprehensive Insight Plus Report. The Credit eValuator Plus Report is a simple credit report with a payment history and credit limit recommendation. The Business Information Report provides a financial statement and business history, as well as the credit report data. The Comprehensive Insight Plus Report adds financial stress and credit scores to the other data. Each of these reports can be ordered directly from Dun & Bradstreet (www.dnb.com).

Be aware: D&B relies on the companies themselves to supply some of the data. So companies may choose not to participate or may supply old data to prevent competitors from having an up-to-date picture of their finances. D&B also does not update profiles on a regular basis. If you purchase a profile with old data, you can ask D&B to update the profile. However, as just mentioned, if the company doesn't want to supply the data, then the profile will remain incomplete.

Your institution may already have a vendor evaluation or metrics form that you can use. You may also choose to weight some criteria more heavily than others. The key to a successful evaluation is to define your criteria before you solicit proposals. Then you control the process and can make an objective comparison.

Vendor Relationships

After you have selected your vendor, you need to manage your relationship with the vendor effectively. Consider this a long-term relationship. Be willing to share information with your vendor to help the vendor best serve you. You can ask the vendor to sign a nondisclosure agreement to ensure confidentiality. Forming a strong rapport with your vendor may lead to a "preferred customer" status or other special benefits.

Make sure the vendor fulfills the contract. Barring extraordinary circumstances, deadlines should be met and quality products/services received. Your contract with the vendor should spell out all of your requirements and the penalties for not fulfilling those requirements. Specificity reduces misunderstanding.

Vendors are significant factors in your ability to grow and thrive. Managing vendor relationships is as critical as managing your customer relationships. Clear communication is the key to managing both sets of relationships successfully. Good working relationships lead to quality products and services for both you and your vendor.

Personnel

"Who will work on this project?" is another critical question that must be answered before a project begins. Projects may have any combination of the following roles:

Project Manager—the person in charge of mustering the resources needed for the project and ensuring that the scope and objectives are being followed.

Project Leader(s)—for large projects, project leaders may be necessary to act as middle managers between the researchers and the project manager. Project leaders assume management responsibilities for their part of the project. They may or may not have budgetary or personnel approval.

Project Researcher(s)—the person(s) who performs the research, collecting and collating the data. This person may also write the report, summarizing and/or analyzing the results. A vendor might fulfill this function.

Project Analyst(s)—the person(s) who analyzes the research, develops recommendations, and writes the report. A vendor might fulfill this function. The project researcher(s) and analyst(s) may be the same person(s).

Team members should be chosen for either their skills or position within the organization. They may all come from the same department or from different departments. Each team member must have clearly defined responsibilities and access to needed resources to ensure a successful completion of the project. The project manager has the ultimate responsibility for the project, ensuring that team members have those necessary resources as well as keeping the project on scope, on time, and on budget.

Budget

The budget, of course, details how much it will cost and who will pay for the project. Estimating the time and expenses for a project can be nerve-wracking. No two projects are exactly alike. Over time, you do develop an intuition about how much time a process should take and what the cost should be. Some people create complex Excel spreadsheets with myriad formulas to reduce the guesswork involved in estimating, but people entering data in those spreadsheets still have to guess at the values to enter.

If you are using a vendor for any portion of your research, he may provide you with estimates based on his experiences with similar projects. If you break down the project into its components and then estimate the time spent on each component, you have a higher probability of creating a more accurate estimate. Table 1.2 illustrates a sample budget for our Welltech Salary and Benefits Benchmarking project.

Schedule

The schedule establishes the time frame for completing the project, typically breaking it down into specific tasks or phases and then estimating the amount of time needed to complete each task or phase. The project schedule may be driven by other events (e.g., a board meeting or the annual budget season). When you chose your methodology, you gained an idea of a general time frame for the project based on the methods to be

Table 1.2. Welltech Salary and Benefits Benchmarking Project Budget

Task	Time Spent (in hours)	Personnel Billing Rate (per hour)	Totals
Preparing Scope and Objectives, Methodology, Personnel List, and Budget	3	$90	$270
Project Management	5	$90	$450
Research—Primary	10	$30	$300
Research—Secondary	20	$30	$600
Project Meetings	5	$90	$450
Report Writing	10	$30	$300
Report Presentation	2	$90	$180
		SUBTOTAL	**$2,550**
		Expenses	$500
		10% Adjustment*	$255
		TOTAL	**$3,305**

*Always include an adjustment factor. This can range from 1 to 10 percent. The adjustment factor takes into account any changes (e.g., vacations, price changes, personnel shifts) that may occur during the project.

used. A project based solely on published sources requires less time than a project using human sources or both human and published sources. If another event affects your project time frame, you may need to select the methodology that works best for that time frame—understanding that the results may not be as useful. Separating a research project into multiple phases allows you to report preliminary results while still using the most effective research methodology.

The other key factor in developing the schedule is knowing how many people will be working on the project and how much time each project member can spend on the project per week. If the project manager or researcher(s) can only spend one hour per week on a project, the project may take a long time to complete. If the project manager and researcher(s) are devoted to the project on a full-time basis, the project will be completed more quickly.

If you hire a vendor(s), the vendor(s) will provide you with a schedule in the proposal. The project manager is then responsible for monitoring the vendor's progress in meeting deadlines and providing useful data. It is advisable to build extra time into your schedule for reviewing the vendor's work.

Once the project is approved, you can create a detailed schedule for each of the personnel involved. As the project progresses, you may need to adjust the schedule. Each member of the project team should acknowledge those changes. If the final report due date is not affected, you do not need to communicate those changes to the board or other audiences for that final report.

Results Analysis and Reporting

After you have finished your research, analyzed your data, and developed your recommendations, you will present that information to senior management or the board for final decision making. Reports typically contain these four sections:

1. *Executive Summary*—Summarizes the major points of the research results and the key recommendations (a good template for PowerPoint presentations).
2. *Scope and Objectives*—Reviews the reasons for and methodology of the study.
3. *Results and Analysis*—Presents the information uncovered during the research, using text or charts, and discerns the themes or trends in that information.
4. *Recommendations*—Applies the study results to the research questions from the Scope and Objectives section and proposes answers/solutions.

Reports may be created in PowerPoint, Word, Excel, Prezi, HTML, or other formats. As you begin your project, consider which format is most productive for your audience. Collect and store your data accordingly. As you conduct your research, you may discover that your original reporting plan may not work. So writing your report as you are still conducting your research may be counterproductive. Chapter 3 examines analyzing and reporting research results in more detail.

CHAPTER 2

IDENTIFYING AND USING DATA SOURCES

Data sources can be broken into two main categories: human sources and published sources. Human source is information collected directly from people and is a type of primary research. Published source, also called literature research, is culled from published or printed sources. Both types of resources can be used in combination or separately depending on the needs of the project.

Before you begin to collect new data, review and inventory the data you already have. You and your staff already may have reports, articles, surveys, statistics from tourism boards, or other relevant items sitting on a bookshelf or saved electronically. You can avoid incurring unnecessary costs if you already own that information. If you purchased a $5,000 market research report, you want to be able to find it for future reference. If you have purchased print materials or saved electronic files, placing them in a central location or library will ensure their use.

Your library can be as simple as a designated shelf or bookcase in the office. Whenever a book or directory or report or magazine is purchased for general use, store it in that designated area. For digital items, create a folder on your network titled "Library" with sub-folders for different topics or data types. If you keep your system that simple, people will be more likely to follow it.

Once you have established your library, think about the key reference materials you need (i.e., books, journals, or reports). You probably already subscribe to industry journals or receive professional association publications. To locate prepackaged market research reports, check websites such as MarketResearch.com or the websites of the American Alliance of Museums or American Association of State and Local History. If you find an applicable report, you can review the table of contents to determine if you wish to purchase the report. Be sure to check the date of the report: one published in 2015 usually means the data were collected in 2014 or earlier. Depending on the needs of your project, year-old data could be out of date.

EXPERTS

Experts can be found inside and outside your organization. Before you begin a research project, think about your employees or colleagues. Have any of them conducted similar studies in the past? Do any of them have experience in the industry or market segment being researched? A simple e-mail sent to all employees before beginning a project could save you hours of research time:

> Hi. I'm working on a project to benchmark salaries and benefits for our staff. If you have any data or know any experts, please let me know. Thank you for your help.

If you don't have internal experts, try to locate external experts. A fifteen-minute discussion with an expert could save you hours of research time. The expert can point you toward resources, answer questions, and provide unique insights. You can identify external experts through the following sources:

- industry associations
- newspaper or journal articles
- colleagues' recommendations
- book authors
- conference/seminar speakers

If a particular expert was helpful, be sure to keep that person's contact information for future use. When you speak with an expert, be prepared to share information with that person. You don't want to disclose anything too proprietary, but the expert needs to gain from your conversation, too. If you can expand his knowledge, he likely will be more forthcoming and available for future contact. Remember: the expert is telling you his opinion based on experience and facts. Don't base your project results on that one opinion. Balancing facts and opinions is key in analyzing research results.

INDUSTRY/TRADE ASSOCIATIONS

Industry/trade associations contain a wealth of material and helpful resources. They frequently gather data about the industry in general; publish directories, salary surveys, or buyer's guides; provide research services or a library; and sponsor conferences. Some associations offer continuing education or professional development classes. As a member, you may access all of these resources for free or at a reduced price.

Some associations also provide news alerts, blogs, message boards, listservs, or discussion forums where you may post questions and receive answers from fellow professionals. Remember, these are public forums, so don't reveal confidential or personal information.

MAXIMIZING DATA SOURCES

As previously discussed, the two main types of data sources are human and published. Human source collection, a type of primary research, is information collected directly from the people. Examples include focus groups, voice-of-the-customer research, expert interviews, and surveys.

Published source collection, also called literature research, relies on information gathered from published or printed sources. The types of material are wide-ranging and include market research reports, news articles, press releases, and company profiles.

Both types of research can be used in combination or separately depending on the needs of the project. Each type of research feeds into the other. Published source materials provide names for human source collection. Respondents in human source collection may mention useful published source materials. Table 2.1 compares both types of data sources:

Table 2.1. Human Source Collection and Published Source Collection Research

Types of Research	Examples	Strengths	Weaknesses
Human Source Collection	• Focus groups • Surveys • Expert interviews	• Up-to-date information • Customizable	• Personal bias • Expensive • Time-consuming
Published Source Collection	• Newspaper/magazine database searches • Market research reports • Industry journals	• Variety of information • Cost-effective • Timely delivery	• Old data • Not customizable

Accuracy and Veracity

As you speak to experts or read articles, you may uncover contradictory or confusing information. Your data are only as good as their source. If you are interviewing/surveying visitors or experts, you will encounter bias. If you are reading newspaper or journal articles, you must bear in mind the editorial focus of the publication. The following five criteria will help you evaluate and weigh the veracity of the data you are collecting:

1. *Accuracy*—Is this information error-free? Does the source use editors or fact checkers?
2. *Authority*—What are the qualifications or reputation of the source?

3. *Objectivity*—Is bias possible? Is the source trying to mold the opinions of others?
4. *Currency*—What is the publication date? Is the information timely?
5. *Coverage*—Which topics are included/excluded in the source? What is the breadth and depth of the information?

If your research is thorough, you will be able to see what is the conventional wisdom on your topic. If five sources contend that a salary growth rate is in the 1 percent to 3 percent range and a sixth source forecasts 10 percent, read the fine print to see how that sixth source calculated the rate. If your data pass all five criteria, then you can move on safely to the analysis phase. Realistically, different pieces of your data may fail one or several of the criteria. As long as you account for those "problems" in your analysis, you still can use that data. The proverbial grain of salt is an essential ingredient in cooking up research. The five information evaluation criteria will help you evaluate data objectively and then use that data appropriately in your project.

Fee versus Free?

When addressing sources, no discussion is complete without examining the question of fee-based versus free resources. Because fee-based content tends to be of higher quality and offer more robust search and output features and a lot of quality free content is available online, the best collections contain a healthy, complementary mix of the two.

Too often, inexperienced researchers spend too much time on free resources in the misguided belief that they are reducing expenses. Experienced researchers know that everything isn't on the Web (or even electronic); and resources that are available for free should be considered as complementary to fee-based resources, not as substitutes. Although some fee-based data may be found on the Web for free, the researcher should consider the following when weighing free versus fee-based resources:

- The authority and accuracy of Web-based data are more often in question than those from a reputable fee-based source.
- Fee-based sources are often more easily—and quickly—searched, retrieved, and stored. And output often can be sorted or otherwise customized.
- Fee-based sources may be more up to date.
- Copyright and distribution rights are clearly defined for fee-based resources.

HOW DO I KNOW WHEN
MY RESEARCH IS COMPLETE?

The completion of the research phase of a project seems intuitively obvious, but it can be complex. Do you have enough data? Are your data accurate? How do you test your data? As you are doing research, over time you will notice that the same authors or data sets or articles or reports are mentioned frequently. If you have those pieces of information and your continued research points you toward those same sources, you have entered what I call the information circle. Essentially, you have uncovered the main information sources on that topic. At this point, you should examine that data. If you have completed your objectives, begin writing the analysis part of your report. If you are missing specific data points, you may need to develop another human source collection or published source collection research tool. You could discover that obtaining that missing data is prohibitively expensive or that the rest of the industry doesn't gather data in the way you want. Or you may need to plan a second research project.

When you think you have collected all of the relevant data, review your research questions, objectives, and scope. Match your data with those questions and objectives. Eliminate unnecessary data and look for gaps. If you are missing data points, conduct additional research. If you are concerned about the validity of some data points, look for additional corroboration. Bad data lead to bad decisions.

During the course of your research, you may have discovered data or points of view that could expose weaknesses in your scope and/or objectives. If that discovery fundamentally discredits the scope, then you should redefine your entire research project. In other cases, you may simply uncover nuances that create new lines of inquiry or affect the analysis of the data. Research is a fluid process. If these data come from a reputable source, even if it doesn't support the outcome you expect, you need to consider the information. It is always best to conduct research without assumptions or expectations regarding the data you will uncover. Insights derived from research efforts should be based on objective information and analysis, even if it means modifying your project or delivering results that deviate from conventional wisdom.

Your research results won't be truly tested until you implement the recommendations. Follow-up meetings to review both the recommendations and the implementation plan as you enact those recommendations are critical. If you defined metrics to assess the success or failure of your recommendations, you should review those metrics at the follow-up meetings.

CHAPTER 3

ANALYZING AND REPORTING RESEARCH RESULTS

ANALYSIS

Your scope and objectives may determine the tools and models used to analyze the data collected. Each category of management issue has corresponding analytical tools and models. Using multiple tools/models elucidates different facets of the data—enabling informed decision making. Part 2 of this book will delve into those details. As you are planning your research project, consider which tools/models you may want to use to ensure that you are collecting the appropriate data.

REPORTING RESEARCH RESULTS

As discussed in chapter 1, as you are writing your scope and objectives, consider the structure and format of the final report, also known as the deliverable. The questions to ask include:

- To whom am I presenting this report?
- How will the information be used?
- How will this report be stored/saved when it is finished?

The answers to those questions will help you create the report outline and choose the media for your report. Options range from a short e-mail to a multipage report to a single PowerPoint slide to an infographic with your research results and recommendations. Your report could be one of the models or templates that are explained in part II; blank versions of the models and templates appear in part IV.

The results of your research will be reported in one or two ways: text or visual. A text report is a detailed record of the project and its results. A visual report presents an overview of the project's scope, key findings, and recommendations. Before you choose a reporting style, first consider your audience.

If you don't tailor your report to its intended audience, your research will be in vain. Your audience must find your research actionable, not simply informative. The board or executive-level staff may prefer a graphics-based report that links research results to an articulated strategy and proposes recommendations to propel that strategy. An executive/board report presents conclusions and recommendations while highlighting the most compelling data, typically using graphics. The executive/board report has four sections:

1. *Executive Summary*—briefly states the management issue, project scope, key research results, and recommendations
2. *Key Research Findings*—summarizes the most impactful research results
3. *Analysis*—explains the implications of the research results
4. *Recommendations*—links results to an action plan

Writing the executive summary also helps you double-check that you have answered the research questions developed in your scope and objectives. It is easy to forget a question or a set of questions. The executive summary could list each question and then provide the answer—a straightforward method of guaranteeing that you have answered all of the questions (or of providing an explanation of why you could not answer a question or questions).

A managerial audience may use the report to implement the recommendations, so they will need more detail and access to the data, as provided in a Word document or Excel spreadsheet. Writing the managerial/staff report first allows you easily to condense the executive/board report. Managerial/staff reports typically have six sections:

1. *Executive Summary*
2. *Management Issue Statement*—describes the reason(s) for conducting the project
3. *Scope and Objective Statements*
4. *Complete Research Results*
5. *Analysis of the Research Results*
6. *Recommendations*

Some sections may consist of one paragraph, a graph/chart, or bullet points. The key is for the report to tell a story—with a beginning, a middle, and an end. Readers like a clear, concise story. Formatting plays a large role in ensuring that clarity. Reports must be appealing graphically to attract and retain the attention of your audience. Well-designed reports have:

- Consistent fonts, heading styles, and labeling
- Labeled charts and tables

- Pagination
- Plain backgrounds
- Simple borders and graphics
- White space

Choosing the most effective visual aid (e.g., pie chart) is also critical to a useful report. Table 3.1 shows you when to use different types of charts and graphs.

Table 3.1. Charts and Graphs: Matching Data Types and Chart/ Graph Styles

	Large Amounts of Data	**Process Structure**	**Size/Share Data**	**Trends**
Bar Chart			X	X
Flow Chart		X		
Line Graph				X
Pie Chart			X	
Table	X			

Too many graphs and charts can be distracting. Present the most relevant information to the audience in a concise manner. You may also use the tools, templates, and models from the rest of this book in your reports. Time is of the essence. Communicating information visually is effective and efficient.

Media Selection

PowerPoint is a familiar medium for reports because it allows you to combine text, graphics, charts, video/audio, and website links in a relatively straight-forward manner. Your board members may be used to receiving PowerPoint reports and express a preference for its use. Because PowerPoint is a very visual medium, you will have to choose the most important points from your research to put into bullet points. You may also have to translate numerical data into graphs or charts. In doing these translations, you may lose some of the context or background information that explains the data. Including more detailed information in the comments section for the slides is an easy way to keep that background information available.

You also may find it helpful to write a more comprehensive report in a word processing program and then reduce that report to PowerPoint bullets. Whichever method you choose, be sure to include the sources of your data in the comments section (in case anyone asks).

Other media may be more effective means of reporting your research results and making recommendations. Microsoft Word or iWork Pages also allow you to incorporate text, graphics, and website links. If your data are primarily numeric, an Excel spreadsheet might be the most effective tool. A video presentation, private website, or a Prezi presentation are also options. Infographics, graphical representations of data or knowledge, can be effective, especially if you want to share some of your research results with members and visitors. You may need a graphic designer to create a powerful infographic.

After completing the report, be sure to save the data sources that you purchased (e.g., books, magazines, database passwords) in your mini-library. You may need those data again for another project or to answer future questions about this report.

Whether you hire a vendor or conduct research projects in-house, an understanding of how the entire research and analysis process works is critical to the success of those projects. The less time you spend on the administrative or process aspects of a project, the more time you can spend on the research, analysis, and recommendations that will help your institution.

WRAP-UP

Research projects and their accompanying reports have multiple parts that require multiple decisions. Although the process may seem daunting or overly detailed, these explanations are longer than your project documents and reports typically will be. The fictional case studies in part III show how project management functions in your everyday processes. Part II introduces and explains the tools, templates, and models that you will use for your projects and reports; part IV contains the blank versions.

PART II

TOOLS, TEMPLATES, AND MODELS INSTRUCTIONS

In this part, we will define tools, templates, and models. We will also learn how and why we use them, as well as their advantages and drawbacks. The goal in using tools, templates, and models is to help us diagnose and ameliorate problems, share information constructively, and identify and consider all of the variables and ramifications affecting our strategies and plan.

Definitions and Usage

As we collect the data that we will transform via analysis into actionable information and strategies, we use tools, templates, and models to impose structure and order in the research and analysis processes. This book contains classic business tools, templates, and models that have been adjusted for use by museums and historic sites, so you may already be familiar with some or all of them. Chapter 4 contains instructional versions of the adjusted tools, templates, and models with response examples; case studies for their use in projects appear in part III of this book; part IV of this book contains blank form versions of each one for your use. If you prefer using different varieties of the tools, templates, and models, you should do so. Or you may also customize them in this book to accommodate the unique characteristics of your institution or department. Over time, you will be able to complete some of the tools and templates in your head, so you won't have to fill out a form. Sticky notes and index cards are helpful when mapping processes or procedures. First you need to learn how to use each tool, template, and model correctly. Then you can adapt it for your needs.

All of these tools, templates, and models are dynamic and useful when applied correctly. Experiment with them to understand their power fully. For the models, ask different people to apply the same model to the same data. Their interpretations of the results may vary, which provides a more complete picture of potential solutions and scenarios. You can also use the tools, templates, and models to facilitate discussions during meetings or to organize your own thoughts.

Tools are used to facilitate the collection and organization of data and information. Like a hammer or saw, if you use the wrong tool for the job, your results will be inaccurate. Tools help you execute individual steps in your projects. For example, you may first complete a Project Charter and Project Budget Worksheet. After the project is approved, you may then use the Vendor Questionnaire to evaluate service providers and the Search Planning Worksheet to conduct database searches.

Templates are guides or diagrams used to organize and display data and information. Templates in and of themselves won't help you analyze data or information. Templates can help ensure that you have collected all of the necessary data and information and are sharing it in an organized or readable manner. After you have collected and analyzed data, you may then use the Managerial Report Template to present your results. Although templates may not capture or organize all of the information and data that you have collected, they do provide a structure that you can adapt for your specific needs.

Models are representations of actual systems or processes that use formulas or analytical processes to predict potential outcomes or assess the impacts of specific actions. Because models ask you to input specific data points or variables, using a model also helps ensure that you have collected all of the data and information needed for your decision-making process. You still control the inputs or variables used in the model and can test different versions of those inputs or variables. Models allow you to generate forecasts or scenarios in a consistent, rigorous, and replicable manner. Think of a model as a kaleidoscope. Each twist of the cylinder reveals a different pattern. Using a model helps you reveal the different possibilities or solutions to your issue.

For example, the GAP Model: Services has you diagram a specific service procedure (e.g., purchasing an admission ticket) and then identify the points in the process where problems or deficiencies either are or may be occurring. Using that information, you can reduce or eliminate those trouble spots. The PESTLE Model analyzes the external factors that affect your museum or historic site. You collect information about political, economic, social, technological, legal, and ecological factors, assess their impact over time, and then formulate your potential responses at the different time points.

The accuracy of your model depends on the assumptions and variables you use. You can create best case, typical case, and worst case scenarios using models. You can also calculate probabilities for each model outcome. Because the calculation of those probabilities can be complicated and requires specialized knowledge, we won't delve into those calculations—a book in and of itself. For most of your needs, assigning a general category based on your experience will suffice: "Most Likely, Likely, Not Likely" or "High, Medium, Low."

Models do have drawbacks. Each model has its own specific inputs and analyzes the interplay of those inputs. If the wrong inputs are used or a key input is missing, the results will be adversely affected. The model may not recognize an important factor or influence, so you may need to add more information or analyses to the model's outputs. Models also assume that people act rationally or logically and that people will execute solutions competently, which is not always true. Models are valid for that moment in time and for the circumstances elucidated. If noteworthy changes have occurred to any of the key inputs or significant time has passed between running the model and implementing solutions, the model should be run again to verify that the solutions are still valid.

Advantages and Drawbacks

If using models, templates, and tools has drawbacks, why do we use them? Tools, templates, and models have five key advantages:

1. Save time and expense
2. Maximize the utility of data and/or research
3. Understand all aspects and implications of research and potential solutions
4. Integrate research results with strategy and objectives
5. Craft well-designed, thoughtful reports and/or presentations

Save time and expense—Structured procedures and data collection plans give you a path to start your research and analysis project, especially if you are not experienced managing such projects. You don't have to spend time creating procedures or developing methodologies and can create a more accurate budget. Customizing preexisting procedures and methodologies should take less time than creating them from scratch. If you are using a vendor for all or aspects of the project, knowledge of these tools, templates, and models will assist in your evaluation of the vendor's work.

Maximize the utility of data and/or research—During the course of your project, you will collect, review, and analyze a lot of data. If you have a procedure for each of those tasks, you will know when and where to incorporate that data and how to analyze it. You also can identify data quickly that has been collected but does not seem to be useful for the project at hand. As you move through the project, you may discover that the data is quite useful or that it is interesting but not immediately useful.

Understand all aspects and implications of research and potential solutions—Simply collecting data and using the forecasting function in Excel does not create an understanding of that data or provide a usable solution. You need to collect the data, add context and interpretation to turn the data into information, and then develop an action plan to create the solution or the answer to your original impetus for conducting the project.

Integrate research results with strategy and objectives—Finalizing your research results is not the end of the process. You need to develop the action plan that applies those research results to the original strategic or tactical questions. The research project may be to collect benchmarking information from other comparable institutions. That information may then be used in a gap analysis to determine how your institution is performing versus its peers. Finally, the results of the gap analysis will inform your strategic plan.

Craft well-designed, thoughtful reports and/or presentations—If you cannot communicate the results of your research project and your recommendations or action plans clearly and effectively, your work has been for naught. The templates and models are efficient structures to display your work in PowerPoint or Prezi or a website, which then may be supplemented with separate text documents or Excel spreadsheets.

As previously discussed, different versions of these tools, templates, and models exist. You can also customize them in this book to serve your needs. Starting points are helpful. Now that we understand how and why we use tools, templates, and models, we can learn how to use specific examples.

CHAPTER WRAP-UP

In this chapter, we learned:

- The definitions of tools, templates, and models
- The drawbacks when using tools, templates, and models
- The advantages for using tools, templates, and models

CHAPTER 4

SELECTING THE APPROPRIATE TOOL, TEMPLATE, OR MODEL

In this chapter, we will review specific tools, templates, and models that can be used to manage projects, conduct research, analyze data, and create solutions or action plans.

TOOL, TEMPLATE, AND MODEL REVIEW

Now that you understand what tools, templates, and models are and how they can be used, you can learn about the particular ones that are most useful for museums and historic sites. For each tool, template, and model, you will get the answer to these four questions:

1. What is it?
2. What does it do?
3. When do I use it?
4. How do I use it?

A visual representation of each tool, template, and model will then follow. Sample responses will be written in italics. Remember: blank versions of each tool, template, and model are located in part IV for your individual use.

TOOLS

Tools are used to facilitate the collection and organization of data and information.

Tool One: Search Planning Worksheet

What is it?

The Search Planning Worksheet helps you think of concepts and phrases to use when searching the Internet or a subscription database.

What does it do?

The Search Planning Worksheet organizes synonymous phrases for each concept you are searching.

When do I use it?

The Search Planning Worksheet should be used when you are conducting a complex search or searching unfamiliar concepts.

How do I use it?

You add words or phrases in the appropriate boxes. You may need to use a thesaurus or a terminology guide to identify synonyms.

Table 4.1. Search Planning Worksheet: *Expansion of a Historic House Museum*

		AND		
		Concept One	**Concept Two**	**Concept Three**
	Phrase One	Museum	Expansion	Construction
OR	Phrase Two	Historic site	Renovation	Building
	Phrase Three	Historic house		

Tool Two: Vendor Questionnaire

What is it?

The Vendor Questionnaire contains a series of questions to ask vendors you are evaluating.

What does it do?

The Vendor Questionnaire helps you collect key information from vendors that allows you to compare and contrast them easily.

When do I use it?

The Vendor Questionnaire can be used before you contact potential vendors by collecting the relevant information from websites and then using that information to create a candidate pool. Or you may contact potential vendors immediately to ask the questions and then create a candidate pool.

How do I use it?

Each question can be answered yes, no, or n/a with comments allowed.

Table 4.2. Vendor Questionnaire: Replacing an HVAC System

Product/Service under Consideration: HVAC System		
Vendor Name: Smith Controls		
Prepared By: Maintenance Coordinator		
Date: 1 April		
Question:	**Answer:**	**Comments:**
Are there restrictions on how the product/service can be used?	Yes No N/A	You have to use their monitoring software; otherwise the warranty is voided.
Are the contract terms negotiable?	Yes No N/A	
Are different pricing or payment terms available?	Yes No N/A	The payment schedule is negotiable.
Are all of the costs (including training, documentation, upgrades, and/or shipping) associated with implementing and/or using this product/service included in the estimate?	Yes No N/A	
Is additional equipment or personnel needed to support this product/service?	Yes No N/A	The monitoring software requires a separate contract.
Are updates/error corrections available for free or for a fee?	Yes No N/A	Free
Have the names of the appropriate representatives been identified (e.g., project managers or technical support people)?	Yes No N/A	
Is there a warranty or other type of service guarantee?	Yes No N/A	Five-year warranty
Can you provide the names of three to five references?	Yes No N/A	
Additional questions?	Yes No N/A	

Tool Three: Project Budget Worksheet

What is it?

The Project Budget Worksheet helps you estimate the time and expense costs for a project.

What does it do?

The Project Budget Worksheet lists the typical staff, tasks, and most common expenses involved in a project.

When do I use it?

You should complete the Project Budget Worksheet at the same time as the Project Charter. Information from each document will be included on the other. Both documents should be approved before the project begins.

How do I use it?

The Project Budget Worksheet helps you break out the discrete tasks and identify the personnel and expenses needed for the project. You enter that data into the worksheet to generate the total estimated cost of the project.

Table 4.3. Project Budget Worksheet

Task	Time Spent (in hours)	Billing Rate (per hour)	Totals
Preparing Project Charter	1	$20	$20
Project Management	10	$20	$200
Vendor Management	5	$15	$75
Research—Primary	20	$10	$200
Research—Secondary	10	$10	$100
Analysis	10	$15	$150
Team Meetings	10	$15	$150
Report Writing	5	$10	$50
Report Presentation(s)	5	$10	$50
Additional Task #1			
Additional Task #2			
		SUBTOTAL	$995
		Expenses	$200
		10% Adjustment	$100
		TOTAL	$1,295

Tool Four: Project Charter

What is it?

The Project Charter explains why the project is being executed, its scope, who will work on it, how much it will cost in time and money, and what the project will accomplish.

What does it do?

The Project Charter clearly defines each aspect of the project and the responsibilities of the project team to ensure accountability.

When do I use it?

The Project Charter should be completed and approved before the project begins.

How do I use it?

The Project Charter is the document that defines and directs the implementation of the project. You should refer to it throughout the lifetime of the project to confirm that it is being executed according to that initial agreement.

Project Charter

Project Name: *Attendance Counting Benchmarking*

Sponsor: *Museum Director*

Project Lead: *Guest Services Coordinator*

Date Assigned: *21 August*

Management Issue: *The board is concerned that the museum is overcounting visitation by including the numbers from the museum director's presentations to peers at other cultural organizations.*

Scope: *Collect and review attendance counting methodologies from other comparable institutions to establish a norm. Craft recommendations for any changes needed.*

Methodology: *Search museum publications and interview staff at five other institutions to collect data. Review and analyze data. Compare and contrast the different counting methods to formulate any recommendations for change in our counting.*

Success Metrics: *Interview completions, interim presentation, final report*

Costs: *$3,750*

Deliverables: *Summary of articles and interviews, interim presentation, final report*

Internal Partners: *Board of directors, museum director, guest services coordinator, guest services assistant*

Risk Analysis: *Low*

Table 4.4. Responsibilities: Attendance Counting Benchmarking Project

Project Team Members	Internal Partners	Vendors
Project Lead—Guest Services Coordinator	Museum Director	n/a
Researcher—Guest Services Assistant	Board of Directors	

Table 4.5. Resources: Attendance Counting Benchmarking Project

Resource	Person(s) Needed	Equipment Needed	Equipment Cost (if necessary)
AAM Publications	Guest Services Assistant	Computer with Internet Connection	n/a
AASLH Publications			
JSTOR			

Table 4.6. Major Milestones: Attendance Counting Benchmarking Project

Milestone	Milestone Completion Metric	Milestone Completion Date
Summary of research results	All five interviews and publications research	30 days after project start
Interim presentation	Presentation of research results to Museum Director	45 days after project start
Final report	Report summarizing research results and presenting recommendations to Museum Director and Board	60 days after project start

Comments:

Signature, project sponsor:

Signature, project lead:

Tool Five: Tree Diagram

What is it?

The Tree Diagram details the objectives and actions needed to complete a goal.

What does it do?

The Tree Diagram shows how a goal will be achieved by specific, real-life activities assigned to individuals. Each staff member will understand what he will do and how those activities will contribute to the achievement of the goal.

When do I use it?

The Tree Diagram should be drafted during the first team meeting where tasks and responsibilities are being assigned.

How do I use it?

Start by writing the goal and then listing the broad objectives that will be used to achieve it. Break down each broad objective into specific activities or tasks. After the team agrees that the specific activities have been identified properly, people can be assigned to execute those activities or tasks.

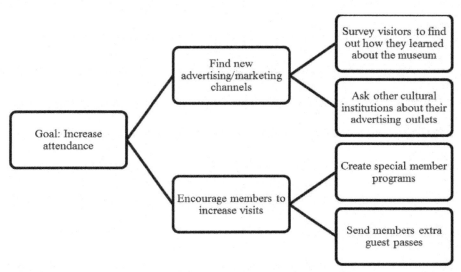

Figure 4.1. Tree diagram: Increase attendance at museum.

Tool Six: Cause and Effect Diagram

What is it?

Cause and Effect Diagrams help you identify and detail the root, contributing, and possible causes of a problem.

What does it do?

Cause and Effect Diagrams build a team's consensus about the reasons for a problem and try to focus on causes rather than personalities or blame.

When do I use it?

You can use Cause and Effect Diagrams when a problem is occurring and you are having difficulty identifying how to fix the situation.

How do I use it?

First define the problem as specifically as possible and then incorporate staff feedback and/or guest complaints to list the causes in sufficient detail. At this point, you are not considering solutions, only trying to capture the main and subsidiary causes for the problem. Identifying all of the causes is quite complex. You should canvass as many people as reasonably possible to ensure that you have uncovered all of the possibilities. Link interdependent

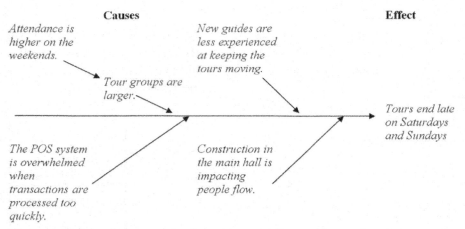

Causes   **Effect**

Attendance is higher on the weekends.

New guides are less experienced at keeping the tours moving.

Tour groups are larger.

The POS system is overwhelmed when transactions are processed too quickly.

Construction in the main hall is impacting people flow.

Tours end late on Saturdays and Sundays

Figure 4.2.   Cause and effect diagram: Tours are ending late on the weekends.

causes. When you are confident that you have captured all of the causes, you can then develop solutions.

Tool Seven: Flowchart

What is it?

A Flowchart is a pictorial or diagrammatic representation of a specific system or a process. Shapes represent different steps or procedures, and arrows show that the steps and procedures interrelate.

What does it do?

Flowcharts help you design the steps in a process or procedure to be as efficient and effective as possible. Flowcharts show whether a process is overly complicated or has redundancies.

When do I use it?

You can use the Flowchart to train staff in how a process should be completed and to detect when staff members are diverging from the Flowchart. Those divergences may be identifying redundancies or inaccuracies in the original Flowchart.

How do I use it?

Flowcharts can be drafted when you are working on tactical plans. Each process or procedure requires its own Flowchart. After they are finalized, you can then incorporate them into training materials.

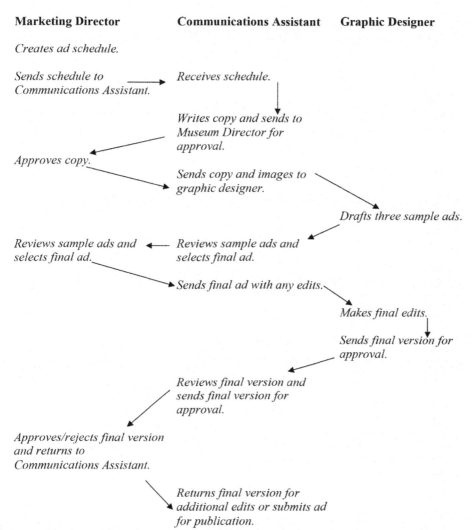

Marketing Director　　**Communications Assistant**　　**Graphic Designer**

Creates ad schedule.

Sends schedule to Communications Assistant.　　*Receives schedule.*

Writes copy and sends to Museum Director for approval.

Approves copy.

Sends copy and images to graphic designer.

Drafts three sample ads.

Reviews sample ads and selects final ad.　　*Reviews sample ads and selects final ad.*

Sends final ad with any edits.

Makes final edits.

Sends final version for approval.

Reviews final version and sends final version for approval.

Approves/rejects final version and returns to Communications Assistant.

Returns final version for additional edits or submits ad for publication.

Figure 4.3.　Flowchart: Ad creation.

Tool Eight: Force Field Analysis

What is it?

The Force Field Analysis identifies all of the positive (driving) and negative (restraining) factors that impact the solutions to problems.

What does it do?

The Force Field Analysis allows you to compare the positives and negatives of implementing the planned change and the human factors at play.

When do I use it?

If your institution is implementing a significant change that requires considerable staff buy-in, creating a Force Field Analysis in a team meeting offers people the opportunity to share their concerns and receive responses in a constructive manner.

How do I use it?

State the planned change. List the driving and restraining forces that will impact implementation.

Table 4.7.   Force Field Analysis—Change Statement: We Will Add Another Tour on Saturdays and Sundays to Alleviate Tour Overcrowding

Driving Forces	Restraining Forces
Visitor satisfaction will increase	The POS system will have to be reprogrammed
Tour size will be more manageable for guides	An extra guide will be needed

Tool Nine: Matrix Diagram

What is it?

The Matrix Diagram identifies and rates the responsibilities and assignments among staff members for a particular action.

What does it do?

The Matrix Diagram visually clarifies the staff and tasks involved in a particular action.

When do I use it?

It can be used to ensure an even distribution of tasks among staff and to clarify personnel responsibilities. The Matrix Diagram does not identify workflow problems within the tasks themselves or the broader process. If you are having problems with the workflow itself, you should use the Swim Lanes Template, which will be explained in the next section, to resolve those issues.

How do I use it?

List the tasks and the personnel who complete the tasks. Assign each person the appropriate level of responsibility for the individual tasks.

Table 4.8. Matrix Diagram—The Action: Orienting New Tour Guides

Tasks / Staff	Distribute and Collect Tax and Contact Forms	Send Orientation Schedule	Review Policies and Procedures	Distribute Tour Content	Introduce to Other Staff	Evaluate Tour Presentation
Human Resources Manager	★	■	■		▲	
Guest Services Coordinator	■	★	★	★	★	★
Museum Director			■		▲	■
Current Tour Guides		■		■	■	■

Primary Responsibility for Task ★
Team Member ■
General Resource ▲

Tool Ten: Blind-Spot Worksheet

What is it?

The Blind-Spot Worksheet identifies the flaws, assumptions, excuses, and inaccuracies that can adversely affect strategic planning or prevent the institution from making changes.

What does it do?

The Blind-Spot Worksheet lists the seven categories of blind spots originally conceived by Michael Porter and developed by Benjamin Gilad. You add the blind spots that occur in or affect your institution.

When do I use it?

Completing the Blind-Spot Worksheet before embarking on long-term or strategic-planning projects can be a constructive way to discuss troublesome or problematic issues that might derail the planning process or the implementation of changes.

How do I use it?

The worksheet can be used to identify biases, sacred cows, and/or misconceptions diplomatically and then discuss their ramifications. It also can be used to identify research projects to either prove or disprove the blind spots.

Table 4.9.   Blind-Spot Worksheet: Visitors' Perceptions of the Museum

Blind-Spot Category	Example
Invalid assumptions	Our attendance will decrease if we change our hours.
Winner's curse	We must launch four new exhibits per year to keep our members happy.
Escalating commitment	Our biggest donor likes our music programs, so we must keep them even though they lose a lot of money.
Constrained perspective	Because we have a small budget, we cannot hire a collection manager.
Overconfidence	Our annual fund-raising gala will always generate 50% of our operating budget.
Information filtering	Our tour script includes a funny story about our founding that is inaccurate but a crowd-pleaser.
Educated incapacity	We have been creating children's programs for decades, so we are experts and don't need to look at examples or best practices from other museums.

TEMPLATES

Templates are guides or diagrams used to organize and display data and information.

Template One: SWOT

What is it?

Strength-Weakness-Opportunity-Threat (SWOT) charts are used to assess the current position or environment of an institution, a product, a service, or a strategy.

What does it do?

SWOT charts are supposed to be generated in response to a specific issue or question and be the first step in a broader analytical process. However, SWOTs have morphed into a template that summarizes the key strengths, weaknesses, opportunities, and threats for an institution, departments, or product lines, which is why it's included in the templates section.

When do I use it?

SWOT charts can be used as an initial step in strategic or tactical plans to assess the general position of the institution or specific departments or products and services. You might begin with a SWOT as an overview and then move to a PESTLE Model or Scenario Planning Matrix to develop a more detailed analysis.

How do I use it?

List the key points in each square with a brief explanation. If you want to use the SWOT as an analytical tool, analyze the impacts of each square on one another or on a specific strategy.

Table 4.10. SWOT Chart: The Museum's Reputation in the Community

Strengths	Weaknesses
• The museum is regarded as a key cultural institution in the city. • Visitation has remained steady at the museum while slipping at other local cultural institutions.	• Community members assume that the museum always will be financially viable. • Membership has declined over the past five years.
Opportunities	**Threats**
• The museum's MOOC classes have been well attended and well reviewed. • The museum's fund-raising has been low key and could be improved.	• Younger members of the community are not visiting the museum or becoming members. • The museum has not received grants for more than five years.

Template Two: Swim Lanes

What is it?

Swim Lanes break out the people and their responsibilities in completing a specific process. Swim Lanes are not helpful for mapping broad responsibilities or reporting structures.

What does it do?

Swim Lanes map when each person contributes to the process, including both guests and staff.

When do I use it?

If there is confusion about responsibilities or a question about the contributions of different staff positions, Swim Lanes graphically show what everyone is supposed to do and when.

How do I use it?

Identify the people and tasks involved in a specific process. Note which tasks occur simultaneously and which tasks depend on another staff member completing a task(s). After completing the Swim Lanes, you can review for redundancies and other inefficiencies. As discussed previously, Swim Lanes and the Matrix Diagram Tool can be used in conjunction with one another. The Matrix Diagram focuses on the broader tasks and personnel assignments; Swim Lanes diagram how the tasks interact in the workflow.

Table 4.11. Swim Lanes: Booking a Group Tour

	Task	Task	Task	Task	Task	Task	Task
Person 1: Guest	E-mail or call to request a tour				Respond to confirmation and submit payment		Arrive for tour
Person 2: Admission Staff		Check the e-mail and voicemail for tour requests and forward to group tour coordinator					
Person 3: Group Tour Coordinator		Check the e-mail and voicemail for tour requests	Check museum schedule to ensure that tour is possible	Confirm tour, number of guests, and payment method with guest		Send reminder notice one week prior to tour	

Template Three: Combination Matrix-Gantt Chart

What is it?

Combination Matrix-Gantt Charts visually display progress of individuals and/or groups toward specific goals and tasks.

What does it do?

Combination Matrix-Gantt Charts establish the project's master schedule and facilitate the monitoring of progress against the time line goals.

When do I use it?

Creating a Combination Matrix-Gantt Chart at the outset of a project communicates the responsibilities and time frames involved in completing the project. The Combination Matrix-Gantt Chart should be updated as tasks are completed or delayed. One drawback to a Combination Matrix-Gantt Chart is the inability to show which tasks are interdependent. You should note that information in a comments section under the chart.

How do I use it?

If you have Microsoft Project or another project management software program, consult the tutorials to learn how to complete the Combination Matrix-Gantt Chart. You can also use Word, Excel, or a sketch on paper. Begin by listing the project's team members, including vendors, and their assigned tasks. Next estimate the amount of time needed to complete each task.

Table 4.12. Combination Matrix-Gantt Chart: New Tour Guide Orientation

Staff	Week One	Week Two	Week Three	Week Four
Human Resources Manager				
Distribute and collect tax and contact forms	██			
Guest Services Coordinator				
Send orientation schedule	██			
Review policies and procedures		██		
Distribute tour content		██		
Introduce to other staff			██	
Evaluate tour presentation				██

Note: The museum director and current tour guides may assist in executing the tasks to ensure that the schedule is maintained.

Template Four: Executive Summary Report

What is it?

The Executive Summary Report provides a top-line overview of research results, analysis, and recommendations.

What does it do?

The Executive Summary Report focuses on the larger strategic implications of research results and analysis to facilitate decision making by senior managers or the board of directors.

When do I use it?

The Executive Summary Report is used for senior management or board reports. It can also be used as the presentation version of the more in-depth Managerial Report.

How do I use it?

Summarize the project scope, objectives, and methodology. Then list the major points from the research results and key recommendations. Writing the Managerial Report first might be helpful, because you can edit down that report into the Executive Summary Report.

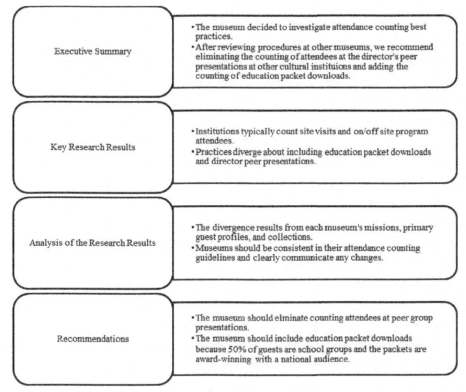

| Executive Summary | • The museum decided to investigate attendance counting best practices.
• After reviewing procedures at other museums, we recommend eliminating the counting of attendees at the director's peer presentations at other cultural instituions and adding the counting of education packet downloads. |

| Key Research Results | • Institutions typically count site visits and on/off site program attendees.
• Practices diverge about including education packet downloads and director peer presentations. |

| Analysis of the Research Results | • The divergence results from each museum's missions, primary guest profiles, and collections.
• Museums should be consistent in their attendance counting guidelines and clearly communicate any changes. |

| Recommendations | • The museum should elminate counting attendees at peer group presentations.
• The museum should include education packet downloads because 50% of guests are school groups and the packets are award-winning with a national audience. |

Figure 4.4. Executive summary report: Benchmarking museum attendance counting methodologies.

Template Five: Managerial Report

What is it?

The Managerial Report contains in-depth results and analysis from the research project, along with more detail about implementing recommendations.

What does it do?

The Managerial Report provides staff with the data and detail needed to understand why a change is necessary, how the recommendations were developed, and the future goals and action plans.

When do I use it?

The Managerial Report should be written at the end of a project. You may then edit it down into an Executive Summary Report or present the Managerial Report to the executive staff and/or board of directors, per their preferences. Depending on the circumstances or board acceptance of the recommendations, you may or may not distribute this report to the rest of the relevant staff. You may distribute it to the rest of the relevant staff after the board has approved the recommendations.

How do I use it?

The Managerial Report is the main document that reports the data and presents its analysis. It is the master record for the project and should be completed, regardless of ultimate distribution. Both the Managerial Report and its supporting documentation should be archived.

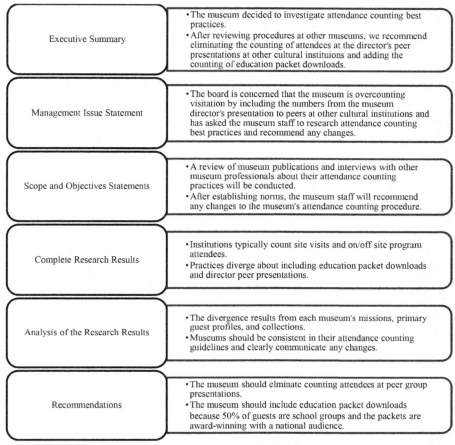

Executive Summary	• The museum decided to investigate attendance counting best practices. • After reviewing procedures at other museums, we recommend eliminating the counting of attendees at the director's peer presentations at other cultural instituions and adding the counting of education packet downloads.
Management Issue Statement	• The board is concerned that the museum is overcounting visitation by including the numbers from the museum director's presentation to peers at other cultural institutions and has asked the museum staff to research attendance counting best practices and recommend any changes.
Scope and Objectives Statements	• A review of museum publications and interviews with other museum professionals about their attendance counting practices will be conducted. • After establishing norms, the museum staff will recommend any changes to the museum's attendance counting procedure.
Complete Research Results	• Institutions typically count site visits and on/off site program attendees. • Practices diverge about including education packet downloads and director peer presentations.
Analysis of the Research Results	• The divergence results from each museum's missions, primary guest profiles, and collections. • Museums should be consistent in their attendance counting guidelines and clearly communicate any changes.
Recommendations	• The museum should elminate counting attendees at peer group presentations. • The museum should include education packet downloads because 50% of guests are school groups and the packets are award-winning with a national audience.

Figure 4.5. Managerial report: Benchmarking museum attendance counting methodologies.

MODELS

Models are representations of actual systems or processes that use formulas or analytical processes to predict potential outcomes or assess the impacts of specific actions.

Model One—GAP Model: Services

What is it?

GAP Model: Services identifies the differences between an institution's perception of its services and the guests' perception of those services.

What does it do?

GAP Model: Services helps an institution determine exactly where problems may exist in its service chain and then create solutions to resolve the problems by exposing five gap points where the institution's perception and the guests' perception of the service process may diverge.

When do I use it?

If your institution is experiencing an increase in complaints about a particular process (e.g., purchasing admission tickets online), or is considering changing a service process, the GAP Model: Services is useful.

How do I use it?

List all of the steps involved in a service procedure for both the institution and the guest. Incorporate comments and feedback from staff and guests. Then review the information to determine if or where service gaps are occurring. The GAP Model: Services provides a structured way to report relevant information from guest comment cards and/or online reviews.

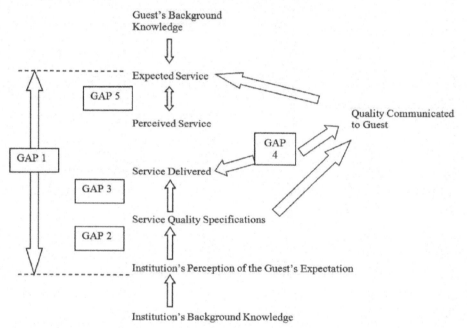

Figure 4.6. GAP model: Services—Guest purchases an exhibit ticket via the museum website.

GAP 1—the processes from Expected Service through Institution's Perception of Guest's Expectation: *Because the system allows the guest to schedule and purchase tickets easily, the institution is satisfied with the process. The guest is dissatisfied because he expects a ticket and a receipt.*

GAP 2—the process between the Institution's Perception of the Guest's Expectation to Service Quality Specifications: *The guest is able to schedule and purchase tickets to the exhibition.*

GAP 3—the process between Service Quality Specifications and the Service Delivered: *The purchasing process should have as few steps as possible and effectively communicate the transaction specifics to the guest.*

GAP 4—the difference between the Service Delivered and the Quality Communicated to the Guest: *The guest assumes that he will receive an actual ticket to the exhibition and is confused when he receives only a receipt.*

GAP 5—the difference between the Expected Service and the Perceived Service: *The guest expects to download the ticket immediately; the museum's system logs the purchase and sends a receipt, but it does not issue a ticket.*

Model Two: Risk Mitigation Model

What is it?

The Risk Mitigation Model assesses the severity and probability of identified risks.

What does it do?

The Risk Mitigation Model lists each risk, its warning signs, and probability of occurrence. You then create a plan to mitigate each risk.

When do I use it?

Risk Mitigation Models can be used in conjunction with specific projects, strategic plans, or general operational/tactical plans.

How do I use it?

Begin by identifying potential risks. You may need experts to help you assess the severity and/or probability of a risk as well as drafting the mitigation plan. Working through the model is also a good group activity. Everyone has a different level of risk tolerance, so canvassing opinion should help you assess severities and probabilities more accurately.

Table 4.13. Risk Mitigation Model: Switching to a New Point-of-Sale System for Admission and Exhibition Ticket Purchases

Risk	Severity	Probability	Warning Signs	Mitigation Plan
The new system doesn't import data from the old system.	Medium	Medium	Data from past member transactions vanishes.	Use different file formats to migrate the old data. Back up the old data in a universal format.
The website has to be recoded to implement the new system.	High	Low	The two systems fail to communicate. The purchasing function does not work on the website.	The website vendor and the POS system vendor have a specific time line with penalties.
Staff members have difficulty learning the new system.	Medium	Medium	Staff complaints increase. Workflow slows.	The vendor is required to provide on-site training and offer additional support after implementation.
Guests have difficulty using the new system.	High	Medium	Guests' complaints increase.	Additional staff members are on duty during a transition period to handle guest phone calls and to update instructions on the website.

Model Three: PESTLE

What is it?

The PESTLE model analyzes the Political, Economic, Social, Technological, Legal, and Ecological external factors that impact an organization.

What does it do?

The PESTLE model identifies the specifics of each factor. Then you assess the current and future impacts of those issues on your organization.

When do I use it?

The PESTLE model is useful when you are crafting a strategic plan or are planning a significant change (e.g., building expansion, major collection acquisition).

How do I use it?

Use the model to assess the success potential of a project or the external issues that must be addressed.

Table 4.14. PESTLE Model: The Financial Stability of a Museum over the Next Five Years

Environmental Factor Category	Specific Environmental Factor	Current Impact	Current Response	Future Impact	Future Response
Political	Congress eliminates tax deductions for museum contributions.	Donations decrease.	Eliminate the language about tax deductions on fund-raising solicitations.	Donations continue to decrease.	Lobby lawmakers to reintroduce the tax deduction.
Economic	Macroeconomic growth and wages are flat.	Visitation and membership renewals also remain flat.	Monitor the situation and respond if visitation and/or membership decrease.	Visitation and membership do decrease.	Prices could be changed. The museum could expand its marketing and advertising to new audiences.
Social	Guests are in older demographic groups.	Grandparents, rather than parents, are bringing children to the museum.	Create programs and membership categories to appeal to these visitors.	Visitation by adults ages 25 to 55 declines.	Research ways to increase visitation from the 25-to-55 age group.
Technological	The cost and obsolescence rate of technology are increasing.	Equipment is upgraded more often, which strains the budget.	Hire an IT consulting firm to establish an upgrade schedule and budget estimates.	Revamp the entire IT infrastructure.	Move to a cloud- or Internet-based system rather than on-site servers.
Legal	Part-time hours have changed because of ACA.	Part-time staff members are working fewer hours.	A workload assessment will be completed in a few months.	Usage and number of part-time staff may change.	Additional part-time staff could be hired; some current part-time staff could become full-time.
Ecological	Improve energy efficiency	The current level of energy costs is too high.	An energy audit will be conducted.	The energy costs may require too much of the budget.	A new HVAC system may be needed.

Model Four: Scenario Planning Matrix

What is it?

The Scenario Planning Matrix depicts and ranks future scenarios that might affect your organization. Pierre Wack at Royal Dutch Schell adapted military planning techniques to create the Scenario Planning Matrix.

What does it do?

After describing and ranking the scenarios, action plans and strategies for each scenario are developed.

When do I use it?

The Scenario Planning Matrix is helpful when you are drafting any type of long-term plans and can be used in conjunction with the PESTLE Model.

How do I use it?

After defining the time frame, scope, and starting point, identify the situations that are most likely to occur and the key environmental variables (like those defined in a PESTLE Model). Rank the situations and environmental variables based on their significance to your institution. Select the two most important situations and environmental variables and then write stories to detail each scenario. Assign probabilities to the likelihood of each scenario and, finally, create strategies and/or action plans in response to the scenarios.

Scenario Planning Matrix
Define the scenario and time frame: *The prospects for the museum's endowment fund over the upcoming year*
Determine the starting point: *January 1*
Identify the potential variables and outcomes: *The fiscal stability of the endowment fund can be either strong or weak. The museum could have a decreasing or an increasing donor pool. The average donation may increase, decrease, or remain the same. The balance of the fund can increase or remain the same. Interest rates can increase, decrease, or remain the same. Given current macroeconomic conditions, experts presume that interest rates will either increase or decrease. Changes in the advisers who manage the specific items in the endowment portfolio also impact the endowment fund.*
Rank the variables and outcomes: *The fiscal stability of the endowment fund encompasses the balance of the fund and its investment portfolio, which is a broader and better measure than simply the balance of the fund. Changes in interest rates have a greater impact on the fund than changes in investment advisers.*
Select the two most important variables: *The fiscal stability of the museum's endowment fund and interest rates*

Table 4.15. Scenario Planning Matrix: Museum Endowment Fund

		Variable 1: Fiscal Stability of the Museum's Endowment Fund	
		Outcome 1a: Weak	**Outcome 1b:** Strong
Variable 2: Interest rates	**Outcome 2a:** Interest rates increase.	**Scenario 1:** Decrease infrastructure spending to save money and to allow the endowment to increase.	**Scenario 2:** Increase infrastructure spending and increase endowment funding.
	Outcome 2b: Interest rates decrease.	**Scenario 3:** Decrease infrastructure spending.	**Scenario 4:** Maintain the same level of infrastructure spending and endowment funding.

Assess the likelihood of each scenario: *Interest rates currently are near zero and were raised slightly last year with little impact. Therefore, the likelihood of another increase is greater than the possibility of a decrease in rates.*

Create strategies for each scenario: *The museum's key strategies are to increase/decrease/maintain infrastructure spending and increase/decrease/maintain endowment funding. Selecting the correct combination may also depend on other variables such as earned income revenue trends, grants received, and fund-raising outcomes. The scenarios above reflect solely the interplay between interest rates and the endowment fund.*

WRAP-UP

In this chapter, we learned about:

- specific tools, templates, and models
- the definitions and uses for each tool, template, and model
- the visual representation of the tools, templates, and models

Tools, templates, and models can be used in conjunction with one another. You may wish to select your tools, templates, and models before embarking on a project or a staff brainstorming session or a staff/board presentation. You may also find that you have to wait until you have collected data or identified the causes of problems before using other tools, templates, and models.

Using them should save you time and money by helping you use your resources efficiently and effectively. In part III, we will see how some fictional museums used tools, templates, and models to facilitate decision making and support strategic planning.

CASE STUDIES

Part III presents six fictional case studies that show when and how the tools, templates, and models presented in part II can be used. The use or order of usage of the tools, templates, and models in each case study should not be considered as the definitive or only way to incorporate them into the problem-solving process. The case studies provide in situ examples of how a tool, template, or model can be used.

The first case study dissects the ramifications of a partnership between two museums. The next two case studies explore personnel issues: case study two examines changes in staffing at a museum store, whereas case study three identifies and tries to resolve a staff turnover problem. The last three case studies delve into specific projects: selecting an online ticketing system, researching and selecting technology projects, and improving a museum's endowment and general financial stability. These case studies will show the applicability and adaptability of tools, templates, or models to the different scenarios: the same ones are used in multiple case studies to show their versatility.

As you read through the case studies, you may think of different inputs or conclusions for the tools, templates, and models based on your own experiences or career level. Consider how your inputs might change the options and reactions of the case study protagonists. Using the blank worksheets in part IV, create your own responses to these case studies or similar situations occurring at your institution. There are no right or wrong answers but multiple, well-considered action plans.

CHAPTER 5

SILVERTON ART MUSEUM AND SILVERTON IRISH HERITAGE MUSEUM PARTNERSHIP CASE STUDY

The city of Silverton had two popular museums: the Silverton Art Museum and the Silverton Irish Heritage Museum. Both had robust visitation, solid endowments, and community support. The Silverton Irish Heritage Museum tended to offer more programs and community events than the Silverton Art Museum, which focused on thematic exhibitions of its collection. The two museums had a cordial relationship but avoided deep interactions. Ten years ago, the Silverton Art Museum had lent a painting to the Silverton Irish Heritage Museum, and it was returned damaged. A dispute arose over when the damage occurred and who should pay for repairs. Thus, relations became cordial but distant.

Anna Hatch, the current director of the Silverton Art Museum, had been a curator when the painting incident occurred. She was always polite to her Silverton Irish Heritage Museum counterpart, Angela O'Hara, who has been the director for fifteen years. Anna tried to avoid deep interactions or partnerships with Angela—still wary after Angela's nonchalant attitude about the damaged painting.

PARTNERSHIP PROPOSAL

When Anna opened her e-mail one morning, she was surprised to see a message from Angela with the title "Partnership." According to Angela's e-mail, the Silverton Irish Heritage Museum had persuaded Belleek Pottery to participate in an exhibition about Ireland's businesses. Belleek had conditionally agreed to loan porcelain, sketches, and photographs to the Silverton Irish Heritage Museum.

"The condition," wrote Angela, "is that an art museum or independent art curator manage and install the exhibition, due to prior incidents. We don't have enough money to hire an independent curator, so Murray thought you could help."

Murray Kelly was a board member for both museums and hoped that both institutions could work together more closely. Murray also knew that the

Silverton Art Museum had a board meeting that afternoon. Though displeased about the obviously planned short notice, Anna considered her options. The Silverton Art Museum had helped other museums, historical societies, and cultural institutions with similar projects. Though people knew about the past incident with the Silverton Irish Heritage Museum, some community members wondered if ten years of frosty cordiality were sufficient.

To gather her thoughts, Anna took out a piece of paper and folded it into fourths. She then labeled the quadrants Strengths, Weaknesses, Opportunities, and Threats and began to write her assessment of a potential partnership with the Silverton Irish Heritage Museum in the form of a SWOT [Strengths, Weaknesses, Opportunities, and Threats] Analysis.

Table 5.1. SWOT: Belleek Exhibition Partnership between the Silverton Art Museum and the Silverton Irish Heritage Museum

Strengths	Weaknesses
• Deepen relationship with Irish Heritage Museum • Give the Art Museum staff a new challenge/opportunity • Incur relatively few direct costs	• Work with same Irish Heritage Museum staff who were involved with past incident • Lack control over the exhibition • Won't have a direct relationship with Belleek
Opportunities	**Threats**
• Participate in an international exhibition • Create a new relationship with Irish Heritage	• Don't know about other incidents alluded to in the e-mail • Could be risking reputation in front of a larger audience

Now that her thoughts were organized, Anna prepared other materials for the board meeting, wondering how the other board members would react to Angela's request.

The Silverton Art Museum Board Meeting

The five members of the Silverton Art Museum board were pleased that the Silverton Art Museum was well respected in its region and were contemplating strategies to establish a national reputation. The main topic of the board meeting was supposed to be reviewing the criteria for the Institute of Museum and Library Services awards. Instead, Angela's e-mail quickly became the focus of the meeting.

"The request does present an opportunity to work with the Irish Heritage Museum," said Anna. "There are constituencies in this community who really want our two institutions to forge a deeper, amicable relationship."

"Yes," said Murray. "We're both important institutions in Silverton and could do amazing things together."

"Yes," said Madelaine Collins, another board member. "The last amazing thing almost cost us fifteen thousand dollars."

"That was ten years ago," said Murray.

"The problem is that Irish Heritage Museum staff is the same," said board member Joel Brener, who was also a lawyer. "The e-mail alludes to other incidents. Sounds like the risk of working with Irish Heritage has increased over the past few years."

"We won't ask you to betray any confidences, Murray," said board member Martha Wallace. "Can you give us a general context of these incidents? Were they as bad as ours?"

"We don't have a lawyer on the board," said Murray. "Angela is more relaxed about contracts and agreements than Anna."

"Terry Connelly is your official lawyer," said Joel. "He knows museum law. You have a well-qualified person who can navigate contracts."

"Let's not put Murray on the spot," said Len Reilly, another board member who was also a former Silverton Irish Heritage Museum board member. "I can say from personal experience that Angela starts work on projects before contracts are signed. Sometimes that works; sometimes it doesn't. In this case, we're dealing with a third party. The Belleek people are business people. I tend to think they won't do anything or ship anything without contracts and insurance in place first."

"How can we protect ourselves from being blamed if something goes wrong?" asked Martha.

"First, we need to decide if we want to do it," said Madelaine. "Anna, what do you think?"

"This project has a lot of positives that will further our own strategic goals," said Anna. "We've never worked on an international exhibition or with a corporate entity to design a completely new exhibition. The staff would appreciate the challenge. It could have award possibilities for the Institute of Museum and Library Services or the American Alliance of Museums."

"We don't want to incur the bulk of the cost," said Len. "We can limit the amount of time our staff spends on it."

"Before we go any further, we should write down and assess the risks of this project," said Joel. "Then we can make an informed decision."

Joel walked over to the white board and sketched a Risk Mitigation Model template. For the next thirty minutes, the board and Anna identified and assessed the potential risks involved with working on the Belleek exhibition, as well as potential countermeasures.

Table 5.2. Risk Mitigation Model: Partnering with the Silverton Irish Heritage Museum on the Belleek Exhibition

Risk	Severity	Probability	Warning Signs	Mitigation Plan
Lack of knowledge about past Irish Heritage Museum incidents	High	High	Already occurred	Require full disclosure, including ability to speak with other parties
Community reputation hurt by not partnering	Medium	Medium	Newspaper columns or editorials; community online forums	Draft detailed response as to why chose not to participate
Problems with Irish Heritage Museum contracts	Low	Medium	Communications from and to Irish Heritage Museum staff, vendors, and Belleek	Have separate contracts with involved parties or disclaimers/ waivers of liability
Poor impression with Belleek	Low	Low	Communication with Belleek	Establish separate relationship with Belleek
First time codesigning an exhibition	Low	Medium	Communication with Irish Heritage Museum, Belleek, and other vendors	Draft and sign off on detailed Project Charter and Budget
Reputation of Art Museum damaged	Medium	Low	Decreased quality of work; communication with Irish Heritage Museum and Belleek	Close supervision and protection from political pressures
Overburden Art Museum staff	Medium	Medium	Decreased quality of work; increase in staff complaints	Clearly define tasks and responsibilities; adjust Art Museum project load

"Happy now, Joel?" Murray asked.

"Can't manage a risk if we don't know what it is," said Joel. "Other risks will appear, but we are prepared for the main issues."

"I really don't feel comfortable voting on whether to agree to the partnership," said Martha. "There are so many unknowns."

"We don't need to agree to anything now," said Madelaine. "We don't know what Angela wants us to do or spend. We do need to decide if we want to ask about those unknowns or just reject the overture outright."

"I heartily recommend that we get more details from Angela," said Len.

"We can't vote on an unknown. It is an interesting opportunity that supports some of our goals," said Joel.

The board decided that Anna should call Angela and determine precisely what Angela needed. Then the board could call a special meeting to discuss those details and vote to either pursue or reject the Belleek exhibition.

ANGELA AND ANNA SPEAK

"I'm a little surprised that you responded," said Angela. "I thought for sure you would reject the request without going to the board."

"Murray's presence on both boards ensures discussion," said Anna.

"Murray's very helpful," said Angela. "I wasn't sure about Len."

"So what exactly do you need from us?" asked Anna.

"Well, we don't perform a lot of installations or even design exhibits. We usually rent traveling exhibits and focus on our programs. So our exhibit design and label-writing skills are pretty rusty. We don't have a lot of stanchions or display cases. The Belleek people have rare photographs and design sketches. They want assurance that we know how to handle and protect them."

"Have you already signed the contracts?"

"We can't sign them until we line up the insurance and resolve the curatorial issues."

"So you want us to design, execute, and install the exhibition for you?"

"Exactly. Independent curatorial and exhibition design teams were too expensive. The Belleek people are paying for display cases, mounts, and label posters, but they need to know what to buy. We're going to charge a separate fee for the exhibition and can offer you half of the gate."

"That revenue may not equal our cost."

"Murray said you want to win an award. This exhibition has potential."

"We'd have to share the award with you."

"Every plan has its drawbacks."

"In this case, we're doing most of the work and sharing half the credit and half the revenue," said Anna. "It's almost like we are simply using another space for our own exhibition."

"Except we have the relationship with the Belleek people," said Angela. "If you are so worried about the money, I can send you a budget, the Belleek details, and our revenue projections."

"That would be helpful," said Anna. "Do you have a task plan?"

"No, we were waiting for your response."

"Send me your documents, and I'll create a task plan."

"Murray said you all like paperwork and charts."

"I've found it makes our work more efficient."

Angela agreed to send Anna the documents by the end of the day. Anna agreed to send the task plan by the end of the week. After reviewing Angela's materials, Anna wrote a task plan using a Matrix Diagram and drafted a preliminary Project Charter.

Table 5.3. Matrix Diagram—The Action: Belleek Exhibition Project

Tasks / Staff	Collect and share exhibition documents	Draft task plan and project charter	Review and approve task plan and project charter	Kick-off meeting with all parties	Draft exhibition materials and plan	Review and approve exhibition materials and plan
Angela	★	■	★	■	▲	★
Anna		★	★	■	▲	★
Museum Boards		▲	★	▲	▲	
Irish Heritage Museum Project Manager		▲	▲	★	★	★
Art Museum Curator		▲	▲	■	★	★
Belleek Liaison		▲	■	▲	■	★

Primary Responsibility for Task ★
Team Member ■
General Resource ▲

Project Charter

Project Name: *Belleek Exhibition*

Sponsor: *Silverton Irish Heritage Museum and Belleek Pottery*

Project Lead: *Angela O'Hara and Anna Hatch*

Date Assigned: *undetermined*

Management Issue: *The Silverton Irish Heritage Museum has asked the Silverton Art Museum to help design and install its upcoming Belleek Pottery exhibition—leveraging the more experienced Silverton Art Museum curatorial and exhibition design staff.*

Scope: *The Silverton Irish Heritage Museum and Belleek Pottery will provide the financing, budgets, artifact information, general project management, and logistics—per their initial agreement. The Silverton Art Museum will provide and be compensated for its curatorial and exhibition design expertise.*

Methodology: *Will be defined after all documents are shared.*

Success Metrics: *On time, on budget exhibit completion*

Costs: *Will be determined after all of the documents are shared.*

Internal Partners: *Boards of Directors, Museum Directors, Irish Heritage Museum Project Manager, Art Museum Head Curator*

Risk Analysis: *The four main risks are: incomplete communications, disagreement about the final design, budget overruns, and misunderstandings about responsibilities.*

Table 5.4. Responsibilities: Belleek Exhibition

Project Team Members	Internal Partners	Vendors
Angela O'Hara	Silverton Irish Heritage Museum Board of Directors	To be determined
Anna Hatch	Silverton Art Museum Board of Directors	
Art Museum Curator	Belleek Liaison	
Irish Heritage Museum Project Manager		

Table 5.5. Resources: Belleek Exhibition

Resource	Person(s) Needed	Equipment Needed	Equipment Cost (if necessary)
To be determined			

Table 5.6. Major Milestones: Belleek Exhibition

Milestone	Milestone Completion Metric	Milestone Completion Date
To be determined		

Comments:
Signature, project sponsor:
Signature, project lead:

Document Review

After completing drafts of the Belleek exhibition Matrix Diagram and the Belleek exhibition Project Charter, Anna sent the documents to the Silverton Art Museum board for comments. All agreed that the documents provided a good basis for a discussion with the Silverton Irish Heritage Museum. Anna then sent the documents to Angela. Upon receipt, Angela called Anna.

"Looks fine," said Angela. "I think the Belleek people will want to be more involved. We're working with a specific liaison."

"Yes, I wasn't sure about their level of involvement and knew that you could add those details," said Anna. "I think we should have a joint meeting with our boards first to discuss these documents and then to vote on moving forward. If we all decide to move forward, then we meet with the Belleek team and finalize the project charter."

"Terrific. I think our board will be pleased," said Angela. "The Belleek people should be happy, too."

Angela and Anna then organized the requisite meetings. After approval by both boards and a subsequent meeting with Belleek, the two museum directors were able to finalize the Project Charter, the task plan via the Matrix Diagram, and a detailed Project Budget and to then proceed with the Belleek exhibition.

<table>
<tr><td>CHAPTER 6</td><td>

MONROEVILLE CONTEMPORARY ART MUSEUM STORE STAFFING CASE STUDY

</td></tr>
</table>

The Monroeville Contemporary Art Museum and the Vernon College of Art partnered on exhibitions, programs, and fund-raising events. Those partnerships typically were successful and engendered a strong relationship between the two institutions. After hearing how other museums and art schools had created work-study programs where the art students worked in the art museum store and the institutions split the wage cost, Vera Kelly, the Monroeville Contemporary Art Museum store coordinator, and Lucille Rooney, the Vernon College work-study coordinator, worked out the logistical details and implemented the program at the beginning of the fall semester.

Everyone assumed that the students would be successful. They could speak comfortably to the original artworks for sale and received extensive training on the point-of-sale system. Within the first few months, customers began posting critiques and complaints about the student staffers. "Unprepared," "awkward," "untrained," "standoffish," and "aggressive" were words commonly repeated in the critiques.

Both Vera and Lucille were surprised. Board members had visited as mystery shoppers and been pleased with the interactions. A museum store manager or assistant manager worked every shift and had not noticed any problems. The students themselves had not expressed any issues. Vera and Lucille arranged a meeting to review the customer comments and figure out a solution.

VERA AND LUCILLE MEET

"I'm not sure what is happening," said Vera. "The comments are so vague. I don't know if there is an issue with checkout slowness, lack of product knowledge, or what. I do have to say that our membership sales have slipped, which I did expect."

Store staff members were responsible for selling memberships; those sales usually accounted for 30 percent of new membership sales.

"The students have told me that they are unsure about how to sell memberships," said Lucille. "They are more comfortable selling art, the other products, and program tickets."

"Over time, they will develop their own techniques for selling memberships," said Vera. "We train them on the products and services but stress the importance of natural language selling. We don't want them sounding like robots."

"Of course," said Lucille. "Because most of them have not worked in retail before, I think they feel a little awkward selling memberships. The benefit is vague. The programs and products are specific."

"There's always a learning curve with membership sales," said Vera. "A bit steeper this time. Judy, our store manager, suggested that we put an anonymous comment box in the break room and solicit comments from the students."

"That's a great idea," said Lucille. "They want to do a good job and seem a little scared to admit that they need help."

Vera and Lucille decided to implement the comment box for two weeks. Then Judy would summarize and analyze the results using a Cause and Effect Diagram.

VERA AND LUCILLE REVIEW RESULTS

Three weeks later, Vera and Lucille met to review Judy's Cause and Effect Diagram.

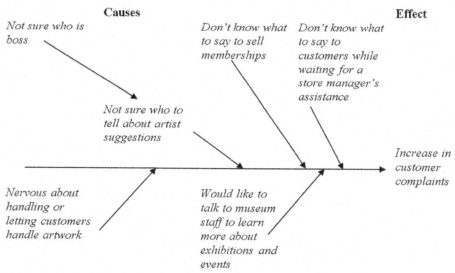

Figure 6.1. Cause and effect diagram: Customer complaints about the staff in the Monroeville Contemporary Art Museum store have increased.

Both women quickly realized that the students did need more training with specific examples of verbiage to use in different situations. Neither Vera nor Lucille had known that the students were confused about whether Vera or Lucille was their boss or that customers wanted to negotiate artwork prices.

With Judy's help, Vera and Lucille created a "What Do I Say?" FAQ and a Boss Question Flowchart.

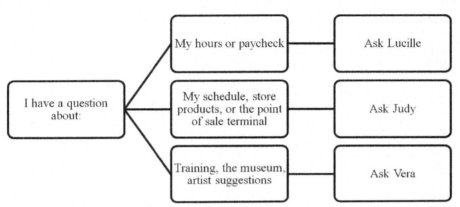

Figure 6.2. Flowchart: Monroeville Contemporary Art Museum store boss questions.

"I think we've answered all of their questions," said Lucille. "This is such a great program. I want it to be successful. When students are frustrated, they usually just quit. I'm glad we are preventing that."

"They're a good group," said Vera. "We've been happy with them, which is why the customer comments were such a surprise. Judy is scheduling some role-playing exercises to help with the sales training."

"Great," said Lucille. "I can't wait to share all of this with the students at the store staff meeting next week."

At that store staff meeting, Vera and Lucille shared the documents with the students. Vera announced that the museum exhibition and program managers would preview upcoming events with the students and be available to answer any questions. The students responded positively to the new training, FAQs, and Boss Question Flowchart.

Because the success of the work-study program was important to the boards and executive staff at both the Monroeville Contemporary Art Museum and the Vernon College of Art, Vera and Lucille created a GAP Model: Services to share with their respective staff and boards—presenting their strategies and tools for addressing the customer complaints and student-raised issues.

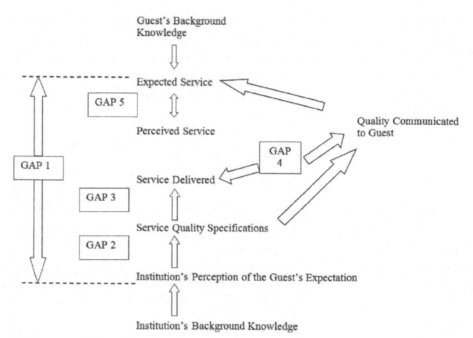

Figure 6.3. GAP model—Services: Monroeville Contemporary Art Museum store staff service analysis.

GAP 1: the processes from Expected Service through Institution's Perception of Guest's Expectation—*We will continue to collect, monitor, and analyze feedback from customers and staff to address concerns or answer questions immediately.*

GAP 2: the process between the Institution's Perception of the Guest's Expectation to Service Quality Specifications—*The student comment box unearthed previously unknown questions and issues. We plan to use the box twice per semester to continue this process.*

GAP 3: the process between Service Quality Specifications and the Service Delivered— *The new trainings, FAQs, and other materials should clarify and explicate our standards, resources, and expectations to the student staff.*

GAP 4: the difference between the Service Delivered and the Quality Communicated to the Guest—*On our website and in the store, we will provide customers with information about artwork pricing policies, returns, and store management staff contact information.*

GAP 5: the difference between the Expected Service and the Perceived Service—*Customer vagueness inhibits our ability to address specific issues. We propose surveying customers now and in two months to determine whether satisfaction has improved. We will continue to monitor customer comments shared via social media and our on-site comment cards, and will conduct surveys twice per year.*

After board review and discussion, Vera and Judy executed the surveys and continued to monitor staff and customer feedback. Vera and Lucille then used that information to adjust the work-study program and edit the training materials as needed. The GAP Model: Services was re-run after each semi-annual survey to keep the board informed about the progress of the student workers, to establish benchmarks, and to monitor service trends.

CHAPTER 7

MENDON AQUARIUM DEVELOPMENT STAFF TURNOVER CASE STUDY

The Mendon Aquarium experienced relatively low staff turnover in all of its departments, except the development office. Development staff turnover averaged 100 percent every two years. The situation became a crisis when the most recently recruited chief development officer resigned after four months. Museum Director Jon Delfini asked Human Resources Director Hedy Beattie to investigate the reasons behind the most recent departures and any common themes from the exit interviews of other departed development office staff.

Hedy reviewed those interviews and prepared a Cause and Effect Diagram for Jon.

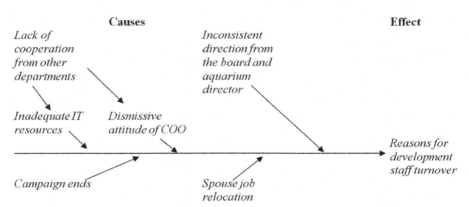

Figure 7.1. Cause and effect diagram: Reasons for Mendon Aquarium development staff turnover.

"So the reasons aren't all bad," said Jon.

"We do have natural turnover, but the most common reasons for leaving stem from the lack of direction and lack of cooperation. Now we have a bad reputation, as well as declining donations," said Hedy. "When I try to recruit for the chief development officer position, people laugh at me. Currently, my specific targets are not returning my calls. Carol just gave notice."

Carol Adler was the Mendon's assistant development officer.

"We just started a five-year campaign," said Jon.

"Carol believes that the campaign will fail and wants no part of it," said Hedy. "I suspect the rest of the staff will resign within the next month or two."

"They can't," said Jon.

"Jon, Roberto [the recently departed chief development officer] is well liked and well respected in the museum world," said Hedy. "You asked me to recruit him to turn around the department and to lead the five-year campaign."

"Which we desperately need," said Jon.

"I know," said Hedy. "When he arrived, he asked for Raiser's Edge and intradepartmental assistance. He received neither."

"We don't have an unlimited budget," said Jon.

"You just spent twenty-five thousand dollars on a board and management strategy retreat weekend," said Hedy.

"That was important."

"You didn't even invite Roberto. He interpreted that lack of an invitation as a clear sign that you were not serious about the development office turnaround."

"So you're on his side."

"I'm not taking sides. I am relaying feedback. I am also saying that recruiting replacements for Roberto and Carol will be very difficult. The five-year campaign will be delayed."

"The board won't be happy."

"Then senior management needs to demonstrate a commitment to solving this problem," said Hedy.

"What do you suggest?" asked Jon.

"At a minimum, you need to persuade Carol to stay a little longer and to take concrete actions to demonstrate support for the development office," said Hedy.

Jon agreed to meet with Carol and try to salvage the relationship.

JON AND CAROL MEET

"I'm sorry that you're leaving," said Jon.

"I doubt it," said Carol. "Inconvenienced is the more accurate word."

"Development is very important to the museum," said Jon.

"Stop, just stop," said Carol. "I don't have the patience or energy for this type of conversation. I agreed to speak with you because Hedy asked. Don't waste my time with empty words."

"I had no idea that you were this angry," said Jon.

"Compared to Roberto, I'm mellow," said Carol.

Jon was genuinely taken aback. Though he didn't think development was as important as operations or education or conservation, he recognized that development was necessary.

"We know we're second-class citizens in the hierarchy," said Carol. "We also contribute 40 percent of revenue. Oh, wait, we've slipped to 20 percent. Too bad admissions or memberships or programs haven't increased to offset the development decline. I'm surprised the board hasn't raised any concerns."

"That's why we're doing the five-year campaign," said Jon. "In your honest opinion, do you think that the five-year campaign will be successful?"

"We use notecards and Excel for record keeping," said Carol. "We cannot run a targeted or cost-efficient campaign."

"What should we do?" asked Jon.

Carol reached into her desk and pulled out a sheet of paper with a Tree Diagram.

"Roberto told you what to do," said Carol. "You ignored him. So that's all we needed to know."

Jon looked at the Tree Diagram.

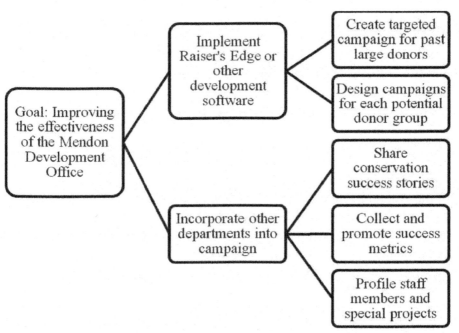

Figure 7.2. Tree diagram: Improving the effectiveness of the Mendon Aquarium Development Department.

"Most other comparable museums and aquariums can do these tasks," said Carol. "Roberto really didn't ask for much. He could have dealt with the lack of software, but Mike's snotty attitude has poisoned the staff for years."

Mike was the chief operating officer. He viewed development and marketing as entities that took resources from him.

"Mike got his penguins, his dolphin pool renovation, and annual board member party," said Carol. "How is that all going to be paid for? I've put up with Mike for a long time. He could not stand Roberto because Roberto is well respected throughout the museum industry. Roberto could have put the Mendon on solid financial footing for a long time. Mike couldn't stand having someone with a stronger professional reputation. You let him be a jerk."

"It was just Mike being Mike," said Jon.

Carol stared at Jon.

"Hedy said other people in the development department may give notice," said Jon.

"I'd bet one hundred dollars that everyone will quit within two months," said Carol.

"That's not good," said John. "How can I get them to stay? How can I get you to stay?"

"If you subscribe to Raiser's Edge and hire temps and a consultant to input and prep our current data, I'll stay for two months," said Carol.

"Just two months?" asked Jon.

"I think you are willing to buy software to make it look like you are addressing the situation," said Carol. "I doubt you are willing to take on Mike and truly support the development department."

JON REFLECTS

The meeting with Carol shocked Jon. He thought everyone accepted his place in the Mendon's hierarchy. The consequences of those assumptions and attitudes hadn't occurred to him. He thought Roberto was going to solve all of those development department problems. Maybe they would have bought software in a few years. Mike really needed more penguins. People like penguins, which should have driven admissions. Mike had nixed the marketing department's suggestion of a Name the Penguin contest, so visitors then didn't seem to know that the Mendon had more penguins.

Hedy had forwarded more interview refusals to Jon. Some board members were asking about the progress of the five-year campaign. The board was concerned about the loss of development dollars and wanted to know Jon's turnaround recommendations. Based on his e-mail alone, Jon realized that he needed to take drastic action.

Jon also suspected that Mike was lobbying the board to be the next aquarium director. After calling Blackbaud to begin a Raiser's Edge subscription, Jon scheduled a meeting for the senior staff.

THE SENIOR STAFF MEETING

Jon asked Hedy and Carol to present their respective Cause and Effect and Tree Diagrams to the senior staff. Hedy also shared the feedback that she was receiving as she attempted to recruit a new chief development officer.

"Top tier and second tier candidates refuse to interview with us. Some have also told their junior staff that working at the Mendon is a career killer," said Hedy.

"It is," said Carol.

"That's enough," said Jon. "This situation has materially affected our revenue, which will impact all departments. In fact, I have canceled all of the individual department staff parties. We will have one all-staff picnic instead of siloed events."

"Why should we all lose our parties because you bought Carol software?" asked Mike.

"Actually, a board member is going to donate enough to cover a two-year subscription," said Carol. "He was so pleased to hear that we are finally making an effort to improve the situation."

"So we can have our parties back," said Mike.

"No," said Jon. "We will have to mitigate the loss of development income over the past few years. We will no longer take money from the endowment or credit lines to cover the gap. Now we are going to discuss the following change: each department will provide material, documented support to the development office. That support will contribute to the five-year campaign and be part of performance reviews."

Murmurs rumbled throughout the room. Never before had Jon publicly rebuked Mike or supported the development office.

"I would like every department head to share their concerns and contributions for this change," said Jon. "In case you need extra incentives, if we don't meet the tiered annual goals for the five-year campaign, each department will have to reduce its budget by 10 percent."

"The board won't agree," said Mike.

"They already have," said Jon.

A lively discussion then ensued. Jon captured the responses in the form of a Force Field Analysis that could be shared with all of the staff and the board.

Table 7.1. Force Field Analysis—Change Statement: Each Mendon Aquarium Department Will Support the Development Office and the Five-year Campaign

Driving Forces	Restraining Forces
Education can contribute success stories and staff profiles	School tour group season has begun, so staff time is limited
Admissions can distribute campaign materials	Admissions staff will need training in how to talk about the campaign
Marketing can help write collateral and share photographs, as well as create a publicity drive for the campaign	Limited staff time
Volunteer management can collect volunteer profiles and recruit volunteers to help with the campaign	Limited staff time
Operations can contribute project success stories and staff profiles	Limited staff time

"Carol, will you stay with us and be the new chief development officer?" asked Jon after the meeting.

"I can't answer yet," said Carol. "Today was a good start. Everyone knows what he needs to do. We'll see if they actually do it and what consequences are imposed for the refusals."

Jon knew that Carol was right. He also knew that he was responsible for monitoring everyone's progress and imposing consequences for inaction. He decided to ask about progress against the goals at his weekly one-on-one meetings with the department heads.

The Cause and Effect and Tree Diagrams had diagnosed the problems and proposed solutions. Jon hoped that the Force Field Analysis exercises had sparked enough staff buy-in to enable the Mendon to turn around its development office and five-year campaign.

CHAPTER 8

FOXFIELD MUSEUM TICKETING SYSTEM CASE STUDY

The Foxfield House Museum was originally the home of a minor Revolutionary War army hero: Captain Fox. Located in the New England countryside, the Foxfield House Museum consisted of the main house, a barn, a few outbuildings, and fifty acres of land. The museum was open from April to November. Annual attendance averaged one thousand people; most visitors were locals who either attended a program or toured with local school groups.

The board and the staff were one and the same, as well as being volunteers. Each February, the four-person board/staff met to discuss the upcoming season, budget planning for the following season, and other topics. For the past couple of years, they had discussed implementing comprehensive ticketing and membership software.

THE SEASON'S KICKOFF MEETING

"So we've approved the landscaping and maintenance contracts," said Josiah Crane, the board chair. "Ticketing is the next item on the agenda."

"We have to address this situation," said Hannah Lawrence. "E-mailed reservations and check payments don't work anymore. People need to be able to buy an actual ticket with a credit card and receive a receipt and confirmation."

"Then we lose the 3 percent to the credit card companies," said Giles Webster.

"I lose more than 3 percent of my time doing the manual processing," said Hannah. "We also lose money because people don't carry cash to buy our booklets and postcards. Our brides also grumble about paying by check. We priced an iPad and Square last year. It wasn't bad. This year, we need at least to have on-site credit card processing."

"I agree," said Hester Wolcott. "I use Square at my store. It's very easy to set up. People can call, and I can process their purchases. My per order totals have increased."

"Fine," said Giles, "but we can't afford to build a fancy website to sell tickets."

"That's true," said Josiah. "Maintaining the Facebook page and Wordpress website is hard enough. Buying a new website could cost more than our annual budget."

"There must be other ways to sell advance tickets over the Web," said Hannah. "You're always complaining that we don't use our AAM [American Alliance of Museums] membership enough, Giles. I can post a question in their Open Forum. Other people must have had the same problem. I'm happy to collect their responses and present the most reasonable options at our next meeting."

"Do you want to make a motion?" asked Josiah.

"Can we make a motion to go ahead with an iPad and Square for on-site sales, too?" asked Hester.

"Are you willing to manage that?" asked Josiah.

"Yes," said Hester.

"Okay," said Josiah, "we'll need two separate motions."

The board agreed to have Hannah investigate online ticketing systems and to proceed with an iPad and Square for in-person credit card processing.

HANNAH'S INVESTIGATION

After the meeting, Hannah went home and immediately posted her questions about online ticketing to the AAM Open Forum. Over the next few days, Hannah reviewed the responses and then stopped by Hester's store to discuss her findings.

"Is that iPad for us?" asked Hannah.

"Yep, it's set up and ready to go," said Hester. "In fact, I already used it to sell a couple of our books. Now I don't have to cut a check to the museum at the end of each month."

"That's great. You're a good sport to include museum products in your store," said Hannah.

"Gives us a couple hundred more dollars each year," said Hester. "We could finally convince Giles to buy a museum computer to track membership on a spreadsheet."

"He would be very sad to give up his index cards," said Hannah. "Even Josiah agrees that we need to be more efficient and electronic."

"They are both Luddites," said Hester.

"I'm glad they aren't reading the online posts about ticketing systems. You can combine program tickets, store sales, café sales, memberships, and admissions in one system," said Hannah.

"Wow," said Hester, "we don't need all that. Can you buy pieces?"

"Sure," said Hannah, "some systems don't have all the pieces. The bigger systems seemed to be harder to use anyway. Trying to do too much at one time."

"I can see that," said Hester. "Giles's head would explode thinking about the cost. Are you going to talk about all of the systems at our next meeting?"

"No!" said Hannah. "I'll have the materials if anyone wants to review them. We're generally more productive when we review one thing at a time."

"We really need to implement online ticketing," said Hester. "Most people have online access or smartphones. They don't like e-mailing us and then waiting for us to call them about buying tickets. I think we are losing visitors."

"That's my concern, too," said Hannah. "We're never going to be nationally relevant. We do have to keep our locals happy."

After her visit with Hester, Hannah decided to build the strongest case possible for her preferred online ticketing system: Eventbrite.

THE SECOND BOARD MEETING

Each board member received a packet containing Hannah's analysis and conclusions.

"I'd like to talk you through my research and analysis," said Hannah. "I posted our question to the AAM Open Forum and received a lot of great feedback. A lot of systems can process admissions, events, store sales, and memberships."

"We don't need all of that," said Giles.

"That's right," said Josiah.

"Correct," said Hannah, "so I took a step back and thought about what we really need, why we need it, and potential issues in implementing it. Please look at the Force Field Analysis on page one of your packet."

Table 8.1. Force Field Analysis—Change Statement: Foxfield House Museum Will Implement an Online Ticketing System

Driving Forces	Restraining Forces
Visitor satisfaction will increase because the ticket purchasing process will be easier.	Implementation and maintenance costs may be prohibitive.
It will reduce already limited staff time spent on ticketing bureaucracy.	We may not have the technical knowledge to maintain the system.
An online ticket purchasing system could increase attendance because tickets are more easily available.	Visitors are used to the current process.

"Your analysis makes sense," said Josiah. "People definitely hate the current system. I don't see how more people will learn about Foxfield because we have an online ticketing system."

"I think we should wait until next year," said Giles. "We just started the Square thing. We don't know if that will work."

"We've netted five hundred seventy-five dollars already," said Hester. "I went to the county history fair and sold a few items in my store. We're usually lucky to make fifty dollars at the fair. With credit card processing, we earned an extra three hundred twenty-five dollars."

"Minus 3 percent," said Giles.

"So I looked at all of the suggested systems and selected the one that fit our needs, which was Eventbrite," said Hannah. "I drafted a SWOT [Strength-Weakness-Opportunity-Threat] analysis, which is on page two of your packet. I think it answers your questions."

Table 8.2. SWOT Chart: Eventbrite Ticketing System Implementation at Foxfield House Museum

Strengths	Weaknesses
• Intuitive interface for visitors and staff • Tools for waiting lists, check-in lists, and reports • Dedicated URLs for each event	• Registration occurs on the Eventbrite site, not the museum website, so people may not visit the museum website. • We would have to export the sales data from Eventbrite to combine with our other financial data.
Opportunities	**Threats**
• Eventbrite shows its users nearby events, which could attract new visitors and increase revenue. • Staff time can be spent on other projects.	• We have no control over the quality of customer service. • Eventbrite could change its terms and conditions or go out of business.

"Our events will appear on this website?" asked Josiah.

"Yes," said Hannah. "My only concern is that people may not click through to our website and may not then realize how rural we are."

"We can refund their money," said Hester. "Eventbrite solves a lot of our problems. We don't have any other systems that would conflict with it."

"Now we have Square," said Giles.

"Have you contacted Eventbrite?" asked Josiah.

"I preferred to wait until after our discussion," said Hannah. "I did draft a Vendor Questionnaire for review—in case we decide to move forward."

"You're prepared," said Giles.

"I try to be," said Hannah. "Please review the questionnaire and let me know if any changes are needed."

Table 8.3. Vendor Questionnaire: Eventbrite

Product/Service under Consideration: Online ticketing system		
Vendor Name: Eventbrite		
Prepared By: Hannah Lawrence		
Date: 15 February		
Question:	**Answer:**	**Comments:**
Are there restrictions on how the product/ service can be used?	Yes No N/A	
What are the contract terms? Are the contract terms negotiable?	Yes No N/A	
Are different pricing or payment terms available?	Yes No N/A	
What are the per transaction fees? How are transaction fees assessed?	Yes No N/A	
When do we receive the ticket revenue?	Yes No N/A	
Are all of the costs (including training, documentation, upgrades, and/or shipping) associated with implementing and/or using this product/service included in the estimate?	Yes No N/A	
Is additional equipment or personnel needed to support this product/service?	Yes No N/A	
Are updates/error corrections available for free or for a fee?	Yes No N/A	
How quickly can the system be implemented?	Yes No N/A	
Have the names of the appropriate representatives been identified (e.g., project managers or technical support people)?	Yes No N/A	
Is there a warranty or other type of service guarantee?	Yes No N/A	
Can you provide the names of three to five references?	Yes No N/A	
Additional questions?	Yes No N/A	

"It looks complete," said Josiah. "Giles?"

"Yes," said Giles.

"Then I make a motion that we vote on investigating Eventbrite as a possible online ticketing system solution," said Hester.

The four board members voted in favor of Hester's motion. The Force Field Analysis had shown that the Foxfield House Museum did need an online ticketing system. Depending on Eventbrite's responses, the board will then discuss the possibility of implementing Eventbrite, do nothing, or look for another solution. The information gathered by the Vendor Questionnaire can be used to evaluate other vendors, as can a SWOT chart.

CHAPTER 9

PALESTRINA FOLK ART MUSEUM EDUCATION APP CASE STUDY

The board of the Palestrina Folk Art Museum felt that the museum staff were not embracing new technology and pressured the museum director to require each department to propose a new technology project. The most compelling projects would then receive funding.

Simone Picot, the director of education, was skeptical of immediately adopting new technologies. She had boxes of CD-ROMs, Beta tapes, and other media containing educational materials, which had not always been transferred to newer media. She also knew that if she didn't keep control of the situation, the board would decide to give her what they thought she should have.

SIMONE AND PAULA PLAN

"Knock, knock," said Paula Van Dyke, the education coordinator.

"Come in," said Simone. "You look very pleased with yourself."

"I've come up with a technology solution that satisfies the board requirement and solves one of our own problems," said Paula.

"Really," said Simone.

"An app," said Paula.

"An app," said Simone. "That will cause us more problems. It's going to be ridiculously expensive to develop and maintain. Are we going to buy tablets or iPads, too? Ten percent of our audio guides are always broken."

"Agreed. Apps are complicated," said Paula.

"How is this solving any of our problems?" asked Simone. "Exhibitions and curatorial have stronger arguments for creating apps than we do."

"Yes, and they are proposing apps for their own purposes."

"Then why would we propose an app? The board is going to be looking for different technologies."

"Not necessarily. The finance committee will appreciate the efficiencies of using the same platform for multiple experiences."

"I still don't see how this is solving one of our problems."

"One of our biggest problems is teachers who don't download the education packets prior to visits," said Paula. "So we have an app that they can download on-site. The kids spend most of their time on their phones anyway. We can have twenty or thirty tablets preloaded if someone doesn't have a smartphone or can't download the app."

"That seems reasonable," said Simone.

"We're using our existing content," said Paula. "We may need to adapt or edit some pieces, but we won't need to do as much work as curatorial or exhibitions. I drafted a Project Charter and Search Planning Worksheet for you to review with Casey."

Casey Whittier was the museum director. Simone reviewed the Project Charter and Search Planning Worksheet.

Project Charter

Project Name: *Palestrina Education Department App Project*

Sponsor: *Palestrina Folk Art Museum Board and Casey Whittier*

Project Lead: *Simone Picot and Paula Van Dyke*

Date Assigned: *undetermined*

Management Issue: *The Palestrina Folk Art Museum board has identified the need to incorporate new technologies throughout the museum to meet the expectations of millennial visitors.*

Scope: *The Education Department proposes to evaluate migrating its school education packets from PDF downloads to an app. This project will determine the procedures, costs, and time lines of such an endeavor to enable an informed decision as to the viability of such an app.*

Methodology: *We will contact other institutions that have created such apps to establish benchmarks and parameters of such an endeavor, as well as reviewing articles, reports, and product literature.*

Success Metrics: *This project will collect the data needed to conduct a cost-benefit analysis to determine the viability of the proposed app.*

Costs: *The costs mainly will be the time costs of the staff conducting the research.*

Internal Partners: *Palestrina Board of Directors, Casey Whittier, IT Department*

Risk Analysis: *The inability to gather accurate or detailed cost and time line data will inhibit the execution of the cost-benefit analysis.*

Table 9.1. Responsibilities: Palestrina Education Department App Project

Project Team Members	Internal Partners	Vendors
Paula Van Dyke	Palestrina Folk Art Museum Board of Directors	n/a
Simone Picot	Casey Whittier	
	IT Department representative	

Table 9.2. Resources: Palestrina Education Department App Project

Resource	Person(s) Needed	Equipment Needed	Equipment Cost (if necessary)
Background Research	Paula Van Dyke and IT Department representative	n/a	
Cost-Benefit Analysis	Simone Picot		
Board Presentation Preparation	Simone Picot and Paula Van Dyke		
Board Presentation	Simone Picot and Casey Whittier		

Table 9.3. Major Milestones: Palestrina Education Department App Project

Milestone	Milestone Completion Metric	Milestone Completion Date
Background Research		Four weeks
Cost-Benefit Analysis		One week
Presentation Preparation		One week

Comments:
Signature, project sponsor:
Signature, project lead:

Table 9.4. Search Planning Worksheet: App for Palestrina Folk Art Museum Education Department

		AND			
		Concept One	Concept Two	Concept Three	Concept Four
OR	**Phrase One**	App preparation work	Development costs	Development time line	App store costs
	Phrase Two	App use at museums	App maintenance costs	Obsolescence time line	App store rules
	Phrase Three	App trends		Maintenance schedule	

"It looks reasonably complete," said Simone. "I'll share it with Casey this afternoon."
"I'm curious to hear what she thinks," said Paula.
"So am I," said Simone.

SIMONE AND CASEY MEET

"Paula is very good," said Casey.
"Yes, she is," said Simone. "We won't be able to keep her much longer."

"Let's solve one problem at a time," said Casey. "The board is very concerned about long-term viability. They hired a consultant to assess our prospects."

"Did you know about it?" asked Simone.

"No. They wanted a non-museum perspective. Someone to look at broader societal trends," said Casey. "The management consultant concluded that our lack of technology inhibited our ability to connect with millennials. Then they gave me a partially completed Scenario Planning Matrix and told me to finish it."

Table 9.5. Scenario Planning Matrix: Palestrina Folk Art Museum Long-term Prospects

		Variable 1: Financial viability of the Palestrina Folk Art Museum	
		Outcome 1a: Weak	**Outcome 1b:** Strong
Variable 2: Technology	**Outcome 2a:** Palestrina adopts new technology and social media strategy	**Scenario 1:** Decrease investment in technology and social media	**Scenario 2:** Maintain current technology and social media
	Outcome 2b: Palestrina does not adopt new technology and social media strategy	**Scenario 3:** Maintain current technology and social media	**Scenario 4:** Improve current technology and social media

"What are you supposed to do?" asked Simone.

"I'm supposed to work with the consultant to write detailed stories for each of the four scenarios and then assign probabilities for each scenario based on my museum industry knowledge," said Casey.

"How? Do you even agree with these outcomes and scenarios? How could the board do this study without your knowledge?" asked Simone.

"Politics is involved. For now, I want to stay focused on the departments' technology plans," said Casey. "My concern is that everyone is proposing apps. If the board says no apps, we're back to square one."

"That was my concern, too," said Simone. "Paula usually has a backup plan. I'll talk to her."

SIMONE AND PAULA PLAN AGAIN

Simone shared Casey's comments about everyone proposing apps with Paula.

"No problem," said Paula. "We can propose a responsive website—it works the same as an app and can be done by our IT department."

"Why didn't you propose that?" asked Simone.

"The instructions were projects using new technologies. If our IT department can already do it, I didn't think it counted."

"How long will it take you to redo the documents?"

"We just have to tweak them. We can do it right now."

Paula opened the files on the network drive and created new versions for a responsive website project in ten minutes.

Project Charter

Project Name: *Palestrina Education Department Responsive Website Project*

Sponsor: *Palestrina Folk Art Museum Board and Casey Whittier*

Project Lead: *Simone Picot and Paula Van Dyke*

Date Assigned: *undetermined*

Management Issue: *The Palestrina Folk Art Museum board has identified the need to incorporate new technologies throughout the museum to meet the expectations of millennial visitors.*

Scope: *The Education Department proposes to evaluate migrating its school education packets from PDF downloads to a responsive website. This project will determine the procedures, costs, and time lines of such an endeavor to enable an informed decision as to the viability of a responsive website.*

Methodology: *We will contact other institutions that have created such websites to establish benchmarks and parameters of such an endeavor, as well as reviewing articles, reports, and product literature.*

Success Metrics: *This project will collect the data needed to conduct a cost-benefit analysis to determine the viability of the proposed website.*

Costs: *The costs mainly will be the time costs of the staff conducting the research.*

Internal Partners: *Palestrina Board of Directors, Casey Whittier, IT Department*

Risk Analysis: *The inability to gather accurate or detailed cost and time line data will inhibit the execution of the cost–benefit analysis.*

Table 9.6. Responsibilities: Palestrina Education Department Responsive Website Project

Project Team Members	Internal Partners	Vendors
Paula Van Dyke	Palestrina Folk Art Museum Board of Directors	n/a
Simone Picot	Casey Whittier	
	IT Department representative	

Table 9.7. Resources: Palestrina Education Department Responsive Website Project

Resource	Person(s) Needed	Equipment Needed	Equipment Cost (if necessary)
Background Research	Paula Van Dyke and IT Department representative	n/a	
Cost-Benefit Analysis	Simone Picot		
Board Presentation Preparation	Simone Picot and Paula Van Dyke		
Board Presentation	Simone Picot and Casey Whittier		

Table 9.8. Major Milestones: Palestrina Education Department Responsive Website Project

Milestone	Milestone Completion Metric	Milestone Completion Date
Background Research		Four weeks
Cost-Benefit Analysis		One week
Presentation Preparation		One week

Comments:
Signature, project sponsor:
Signature, project lead:

Table 9.9. Search Planning Worksheet: Responsive Website for Palestrina Folk Art Museum Education Department

		Concept One	Concept Two	Concept Three
	Phrase One	Responsive website preparation work	Development costs	Development time line
OR	Phrase Two	Responsive website use at museums	Responsive website maintenance costs	Obsolescence time line
	Phrase Three	Responsive website trends		Maintenance schedule

AND

Simone sent the revised documents to Casey for the upcoming board meeting. Although she was confident that she and Paula were prepared to execute whichever project was selected, Simone was anxious about the results of the Scenario Planning Matrix and its impact on the Palestrina's immediate and long-term future. Simone had seen consultants use such analyses and models to persuade boards to make changes without considering practicalities and consequences. She hoped that wouldn't happen at the Palestrina but decided to update her resume—just in case.

CHAPTER 10

GOOSE HOLLOW ARTS AND SCIENCES MUSEUM FINANCIAL STABILITY CASE STUDY

The Goose Hollow Arts and Sciences Museum was located in Goose Hollow, the county seat in largely rural Crane County. The museum served Goose Hollow County and other surrounding counties within a radius of two hundred miles. The annual budget was funded 25 percent from the state, 25 percent from the endowment, 20 percent from the county, and the remaining 30 percent from the museum's earned income. After the recent economic downturn, the endowment decreased 30 percent, and the state cut its funding in half. The county was maintaining its 20 percent contribution but had warned Museum Director Edwin Avery that its contribution may be reduced in the upcoming fiscal year.

Through discussions with his fellow museum directors, Edwin had learned that they too were challenged with double-digit reductions in state funding, endowment income, grants, and/or donations. Edwin scheduled a meeting with Alexandra Coonley, his development coordinator.

EDWIN AND ALEXANDRA MEET

"I'm glad you asked for a special meeting," said Alexandra. "I'm worried about our level of donations and the board's non-reaction to the problem."

"You have to understand," said Edwin, "that most of the board members inherited their seats and view their membership as a noblesse oblige obligation. They mean well but are happier attending openings than planning strategy."

"That doesn't help us now," said Alexandra. "I thought most of them were friends with state legislators. Why can't they nudge their friends to maintain our funding?"

"As much as people support museums, they prefer spending state funds on health care or schools," said Edwin. "When money is plentiful, everyone can share in the wealth. When the money dries up, you have to ration. Two other museums have had to close because more than half of their funding was from the state."

"I know! That's what scares me. We need to scare the board," said Alexandra. "I know they want to stick their heads in the sand, but we need to take action now to avoid deep cuts or even closure."

"I agree. Fear paralyzes them. I think that a more rational packaging could prod them into making some decisions—including increasing their own contributions and being more active fund-raisers," said Edwin.

"That's true," said Alexandra. "They do the bare minimum now."

"I want to inspire them to do more," said Edwin. "I prepared a PESTLE [Political, Economic, Social, Technological, Legal, and Ecological] Model to show the different factors that impact the museum and put the economic factors in context with other issues. Take a look. What do you think?"

Edwin handed the PESTLE to Alexandra, who read the paper.

Table 10.1. PESTLE Model: The Financial Stability of the Goose Hollow Arts and Sciences Museum over the Next Five Years

Environmental Factor Category	Specific Environmental Factor	Current Impact	Current Response	Future Impact	Future Response
Political	Reduced state and county funding	Budget shortfall of 10%	Reduce administrative costs	Identify additional revenue sources	Implement fund-raising campaign to increase endowment
Economic	Overall, multiyear economic recession	Endowment investment has decreased	Monitor investment performance as economy improves	Endowment returns remain suboptimal	Reevaluate endowment investment portfolio
Social	Aging visitor demographics	Attendance is declining	Interview visitors about reasons for visiting and museum experience	Attendance flattens	Create programs and exhibits to appeal to specific age groups
Technological	The cost and obsolescence rate of technology are increasing	We cannot afford to upgrade our technology	Stagger upgrading/ updating schedule— prioritizing guest-facing technologies	Support hardware and software of multiple generations	Need more IT help or eventually replace all systems
Legal	Mandatory minimum wage increase passed	Higher labor costs are incurred	Use more part-time or volunteer workers	Usage and number of part-time staff may change fundamentally	The guest experience may be negatively impacted
Ecological	Maintain our one hundred acres	The current level of costs is 15% of our budget	We must maintain because of the land trust	The costs may require an even greater share of the budget	More financial resources will be needed

"I think it looks good," said Alexandra. "I can't think of any edits right now, but let me sit with it for a little while."

"The board meeting is next week, so we have plenty of time," said Edwin. "I want to share some articles about the state's budget process and issues at other museums, too. I'll prepare the packets next Wednesday, so just send your edits by then."

Edwin and Alexandra continued meeting: discussing different fund-raising strategies, opportunities for grant applications, and possible big donor targets.

EDWIN PREPARES FOR THE BOARD MEETING

As the board meeting neared, Edwin knew that he would have to keep the board focused on the potentially dire future financial predicament and supporting increased fund-raising requirements. He decided to create a Risk Mitigation Model and a Blind-Spot Worksheet to keep the board on task.

Table 10.2. Risk Mitigation Model: Increasing Goose Hollow Arts and Sciences Museum's Fund-raising Goals

Risk	Severity	Probability	Warning Signs	Mitigation Plan
The development office doesn't have enough staff	Low	Low	Staff requires overtime	Monitor time sheets and consider the use of temporary staff
The board doesn't support the new goals	High	Medium	The board approves new levels or doesn't contribute at the new levels	Reconsider board requirements
Campaign costs overrun	High	Low	Campaign spending outpaces the campaign budget	Reevaluate campaign tactics and budget
Campaign does not meet goals	High	Medium	Donations are less than the milestone goals	Identify larger potential donor pool; ask large donors to participate in a matching program

Table 10.3. Blind-Spot Worksheet: Goose Hollow Arts and Sciences Museum Viability

Blind-Spot Category	Goose Hollow Blind Spot
Invalid Assumptions	We are a valued community institution that will always receive government funding.
Winner's Curse	We must give free admission to government officials and their families to ensure their support.
Escalating Commitment	We cannot increase board fund-raising requirements because people won't want to serve on the board.
Constrained Perspective	We have multiple revenue sources and therefore do not need to investigate new revenue sources.
Overconfidence	Our donations will return to prerecession levels because we are a valued community institution.
Information Filtering	Our donations are a direct reflection of our place in the community.
Educated Incapacity	We have been government supported for decades and will continue to be so.

Edwin believed that he had prepared all of the documents he could to help the board have a productive discussion about Goose Hollow's financial future. He hoped the board would react accordingly.

THE BOARD MEETING

As the board members entered the meeting room, Edwin handed each of them a packet. For the first fifteen minutes, the board read the materials.

"Quite a bit to ponder," said board chair Quentin Lloyd.

"It is," said Edwin. "We don't have to make a lot of decisions today. If we can prioritize issues and assign board subcommittees to do additional research or draft plans, we will have accomplished a lot."

"Shouldn't the museum staff be handling these issues?" asked Frances Richardson, another board member. "They're paid to manage the museum."

"We're supposed to set the overall strategic goals and to provide advice," said Quentin. "We don't just show up to the parties and receive the congratulations for other people's work."

"We should be speaking with our friends who can donate or lobby state legislators," said Sinclair Steinbeck, another board member. "The museum staff is supposed to share this information with us, so we can help."

"This could take years," said Frances.

"Then we should start now," said Sinclair.

"It seems like you are expecting the board members' donations to replace the temporarily reduced government funding," said Quentin.

"We're not made of money," said Frances.

"I would hope that the board would set an example by increasing its donations and explaining to the community that they are increasing their donations because of the reduced government contribution," said Edwin. "Frankly, I think we should assume that we will not see that level of funding again."

"I agree," said Sinclair. "Think of how much money we lose comping all of those admission and program tickets to politicians and their families. They need to pay."

"That's why I prepared these documents—to spark the conversation. If you have any questions or other points of view or disagreements with the documents, we should discuss them," said Edwin. "We always prepare materials to guide and inform the board's decisions. If you feel that we have misinterpreted, overstated, or understated a scenario or risk, this is the time to consider other points of view. I know it's a lot to take in. We do need to start these conversations."

"Right, we can't resolve all of these issues in the next hour," said Sinclair. "We need to figure out what we can decide now and what we need to research."

"Let's review each document closely and go from there," said Quentin.

After ninety minutes of spirited discussion, Edwin and the board had analyzed the information in each document and developed action plans for the key items. Although Goose Hollow's problems were not resolved that afternoon, Edwin and the board did have a manageable, achievable framework in order to proceed.

EPILOGUE

These six case studies show how tools, templates, and models can be used to broach or guide difficult discussions. Inviting participants to create or edit these documents provides everyone with an opportunity to share his or her point of view constructively and productively. People may still disagree about interpretations, weightings, analyses, or conclusions. Tools, templates, and models can capture those disagreements and turn them into useful, counter-balanced data.

PART IV

TOOLS, TEMPLATES, AND MODELS WORKSHEETS

This part of the book provides blank versions of the tools, templates, and models that were defined and exemplified in the first three parts of this book. Instructions and estimated completion times are also provided. If you are familiar with a particular tool, template, or model, you may be able to complete the worksheet quickly. If your project is very complex or requires consultation with other people, you may need more time to complete the relevant worksheets. The first time you use a tool, template, or model, you may spend extra time reviewing the other examples in this book or in other resources before completing the worksheet. All of these tools, templates, and models were created to improve our efficiency and to reduce time spent on such activities by providing a replicable methodology to help you achieve your goals and objectives. Spend your time achieving those goals and objectives, not overthinking these worksheets. You may choose to complete these tools, templates, and models as a group, too.

Remember—part II answered the following questions for each tool, template, and model:

- What is it?
- What does it do?
- When do I use it?
- How do I use it?

These versions should meet most needs. As previously discussed, you may need to modify a tool, template, or model to fit the circumstances of your project or institution. You may need to add another person or task to the tool, template, or model. When in doubt, use these versions first and then adapt when necessary. Although all of these tools, templates, and models are flexible and scalable to adjust to your individual circumstances, the four models and the Blind-Spot Worksheet are the only items whose basic structures and functions cannot be adapted, changed, or customized.

CHAPTER 11

TOOLS, TEMPLATES, AND MODELS WORKSHEETS

TOOL ONE: SEARCH PLANNING WORKSHEET

Instructions: Write down the topic of your search. Break the topic into between one and four main concepts. Then define each of those key concepts as one- to three-word phrases. List the key concepts at the top of each column. Then add between one and four synonym phrases for each concept. Use those concepts/keywords as you search the Internet or a database. As you perform your search, you may uncover other concepts or synonyms. Simply add those items to the worksheet and rerun your search.

Completion Time: five to ten minutes

Table 11.1.   Search Planning Worksheet

Topic:

		Concept One	Concept Two	Concept Three
		AND		
	Phrase One			
OR	**Phrase Two**			
	Phrase Three			

TOOL TWO: VENDOR QUESTIONNAIRE

Instructions: Review the questions below. You may need to reword them or include additional questions, depending on the product or service under consideration. You also may want to review the questionnaire with experts (e.g., the IT department, a lawyer, the curatorial department) to ensure that you are asking the appropriate questions. Then contact the vendors under consideration. You may send them your questionnaire for completion or speak with them over the phone and transcribe their answers.

Completion Time: both the question review and questionnaire completion may take fifteen minutes to several hours.

Table 11.2. Vendor Questionnaire

Topic:

Product/Service under Consideration:		
Vendor Name:		
Prepared By:		
Date:		
Question:	**Answer:**	**Comments**
Are there restrictions on how the product/service can be used?	Yes No N/A	
Are the contract terms negotiable?	Yes No N/A	
Are different pricing or payment terms available?	Yes No N/A	
Are all of the costs (including training, documentation, upgrades, and/or shipping) associated with implementing and/or using this product/service included in the estimate?	Yes No N/A	
Is additional equipment or personnel needed to support this product/service?	Yes No N/A	
Are updates/error corrections available for free or for a fee?	Yes No N/A	
Have the names of the appropriate representatives been identified (e.g., project managers or technical support people)?	Yes No N/A	

Is there a warranty or other type of service guarantee?	Yes No N/A	
Can you provide the names of three to five references?	Yes No N/A	
Additional questions?	Yes No N/A	

TOOL THREE: PROJECT BUDGET WORKSHEET

Instructions: Break down the project into discrete tasks. The example below captures the key tasks for a typical project. Adjust accordingly for your project. Consider how many people will be needed to perform each task and how much time will be required to complete each task. Even if you are not sure of the exact amount of time, do your best to estimate the hours needed. Multiply those hours by an internal or external billing rate to determine the project budget. Be sure to total the number of hours as well, to assist in the creation of the project schedule. The 10 percent adjustment is 10 percent of the project subtotal and is added to provide an estimate of potential cost overruns or other unexpected events.

Completion Time: fifteen to sixty minutes

Table 11.3.   Project Budget Worksheet

Project Name:

Task	Time Spent (in hours)	Billing Rate (per hour, in $)	Totals
Preparing Project Charter			
Project Management			
Vendor Management			
Research—Primary			
Research—Secondary			
Analysis			
Team Meetings			
Report Writing			
Report Presentation(s)			
Additional Task #1			
Additional Task #2			
		SUBTOTAL	
		Expenses	
		10% Adjustment	
		TOTAL	

TOOL FOUR: PROJECT CHARTER

Instructions: Complete each of the line items below. The sponsor is the person or entity (e.g., the board of directors) who has requested the project; the project lead is the person who will manage the project. The Management Issue asks you to explicate the management issue that the project is supporting and then to describe how the project will align with or resolve specific objectives. The Scope defines what the project will do. Methodology details how you will execute the project; Success Metrics describes how you will determine the success of the project. Use Risk Analysis to identify factors that could compromise the project's success and to craft a risk mitigation strategy. For the tables, you may need to add more columns or rows for your particular project.

Completion Time: one to three hours

Project Charter
Project Name:
Sponsor:
Project Lead:
Date Assigned:
Management Issue:
Scope:
Methodology:
Success Metrics:
Costs:
Deliverables:
Internal Partners:
Risk Analysis:

Table 11.4. Responsibilities

Project Team Members	Internal Partners	Vendors

Table 11.5. Resources

Resource	Person(s) Needed	Equipment Needed	Equipment Cost (if necessary)

Table 11.6. Major Milestones

Milestone	Milestone Completion Metric	Milestone Completion Date

Comments:

Signature and Date, project sponsor:

Signature and Date, project lead:

TOOL FIVE: TREE DIAGRAM

Instructions: Write down your goal. List the objectives that will support the goal. Define the specific activities that will be used to execute the objectives.

Completion Time: fifteen to sixty minutes

Project Goal:

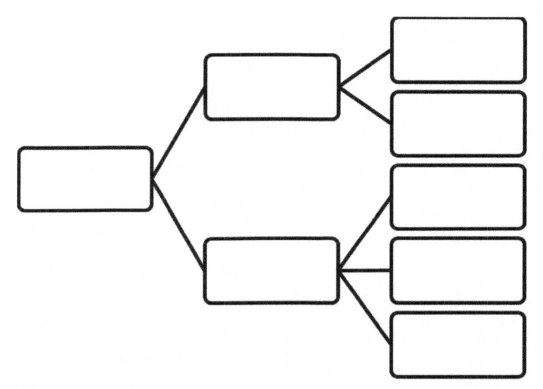

Figure 11.1. Tree diagram.

TOOL SIX: CAUSE AND EFFECT DIAGRAM

Instructions: Define your problem, the "effect," as specifically and detailed as possible. Then list all of the causes that lead to the problem. Those causes may be gleaned from guest and/or staff feedback. Group interrelated causes. This activity is best completed over several days to ensure that you are capturing all of the causes at their most specific.

Completion Time: one to four hours, over one to seven days

Topic:

Causes   Effect

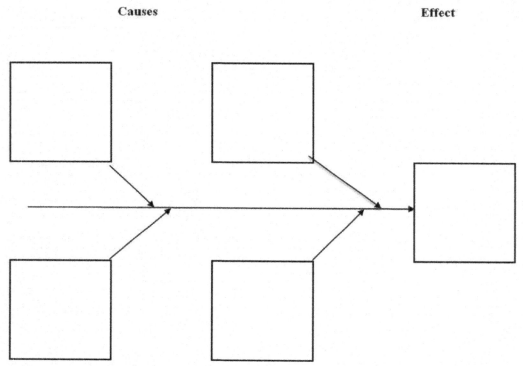

Figure 11.2. Cause and effect diagram.

TOOL SEVEN: FLOWCHART

Given the nature of the flowchart, creating a blank, universal version is difficult. The representations below provide two examples of how a flowchart is constructed.

Instructions: Identify the process or procedure to analyze. List all of the personnel and their individual activities that support that process or procedure. Use arrows to show the completion order of each activity. Then analyze the chart for discrepancies and redundancies.

Completion Time: one-half hour to two hours

Topic:

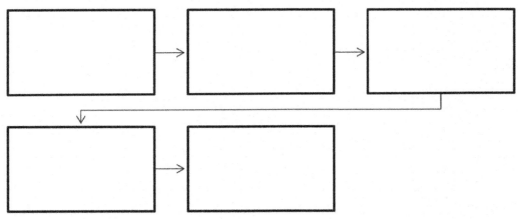

Figure 11.3. Flowchart version 1.

or

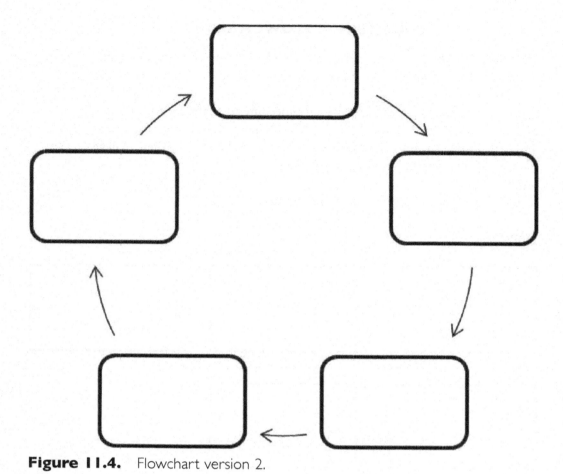

Figure 11.4. Flowchart version 2.

TOOL EIGHT: FORCE FIELD ANALYSIS

Instructions: Write down your change statement. As individuals or in a meeting, list the driving and restraining forces that will affect the implementation of the change.

Completion Time: thirty to sixty minutes

Table 11.7. Force Field Analysis: Change Statement

Driving Forces	Restraining Forces

TOOL NINE: MATRIX DIAGRAM

Instructions: Identify the action or activity to be executed. List the staff and the tasks involved in completing the action or activity. Assign each person the appropriate level of responsibility (primary, team member, general resource, or none) for each task.

Completion Time: fifteen to sixty minutes

Table 11.8. Matrix Diagram

The Action:

Tasks Staff	Task 1	Task 2	Task 3	Task 4	Task 5	Task 6
Person 1						
Person 2						
Person 3						
Person 4						

Primary Responsibility for Task ★
Team Member ■
General Resource ▲

TOOL TEN: BLIND-SPOT WORKSHEET

Instructions: Write down the topic of your analysis. List as many examples of blind spots in their relevant categories. The focus should be on identifying the blind spots. Then you may assign risk factors (high, medium, low) to each specific blind spot and craft strategies and tactics to reduce the impact of the high- and/or medium-level blind spots. This exercise may be completed as a group or as individuals and then merged into a group document.

Completion Time: one-half hour to two hours

Table 11.9. Blind-Spot Worksheet

Topic:

Blind-Spot Category	Example
Invalid Assumptions	
Winner's Curse	
Escalating Commitment	
Constrained Perspective	
Overconfidence	
Information Filtering	
Educated Incapacity	

TEMPLATE ONE: SWOT

Instructions: Select and define the topic or issue to analyze. In the Strengths and Weaknesses boxes, list the strengths and weaknesses of the topic or issue from the point of view of your institution. In the Opportunities and Threats, list the opportunities and threats from outside your institution that impact the topic or issue under analysis. Depending on the complexity of topic or issue, a simple bulleted list may suffice. In other situations, you may need to write one or several paragraphs for each of the points in each of the boxes, which may be included beneath the box diagram if you prefer. You may also weight the probability of the likelihood of each item occurring in each box.

Completion Time: one-half hour to four hours

Table 11.10. SWOT Chart

Topic:

Strengths	Weaknesses
Opportunities	**Threats**

TEMPLATE TWO: SWIM LANES

Instructions: Write down the operational process under analysis. Identify each person who works on the process. Describe the task each person performs. Make sure that simultaneous tasks are recorded in the same column and that dependent tasks are properly recorded in the rows. Analyze the swim lanes for inefficiencies and redundancies.

Completion Time: one-half hour to two hours

Table 11.11.   Swim Lanes

Project:

	Task	Task	Task	Task	Task	Task	Task
Person 1							
Person 2							
Person 3							

TEMPLATE THREE:
COMBINATION MATRIX-GANTT CHART

Instructions: List the team members, tasks, and time lines for a project. Be sure to include vendors and/or item deliveries. Estimate the amount of time to complete each task. Shade the appropriate cell to indicate when the responsible person will be completing that task.

Completion Time: thirty to sixty minutes

Table 11.12.   Combination Matrix-Gantt Chart

Project:

Staff	Week One	Week Two	Week Three	Week Four
Person 1				
Task 1				
Person 2				
Task 2				
Task 3				

Person 3				
Task 4				
Task 5				

TEMPLATE FOUR: EXECUTIVE SUMMARY REPORT

Instructions: Summarize the project scope, objective, and methodology. List the major discoveries uncovered during the research phase of the project and the key recommendations. If you wrote a Managerial Report, use that report to complete this template. If you are only writing an Executive Summary, you may want to include research results or other materials in appendixes to assist readers.

Completion Time: one to three hours

Title:

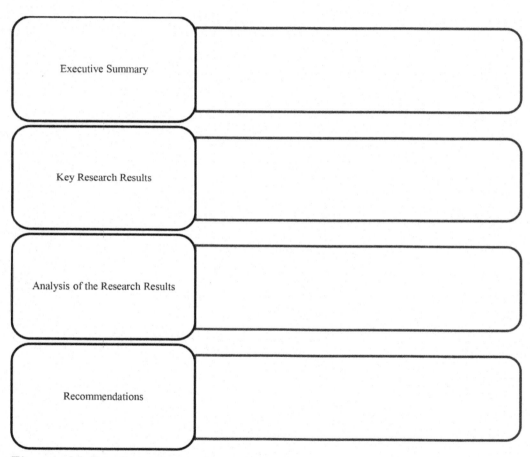

Executive Summary	
Key Research Results	
Analysis of the Research Results	
Recommendations	

Figure 11.5. Executive summary report.

TEMPLATE FIVE: MANAGERIAL REPORT

Instructions: Begin by reiterating the Management Issue, Scope, and Objectives. Explain and share the complete results from your research, including citing sources or quoting experts. Analyze those results and describe how the results support or oppose the management issue, as well as other relevant institutional strategies. Craft Recommendations for your institution to implement, including action plans to implement the Recommendations, if possible. Then write the Executive Summary.

Completion Time: three to six hours

Title:

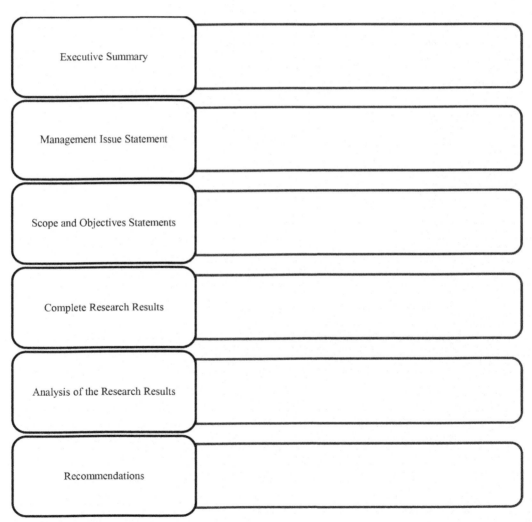

Executive Summary	
Management Issue Statement	
Scope and Objectives Statements	
Complete Research Results	
Analysis of the Research Results	
Recommendations	

Figure 11.6. Managerial report.

MODEL ONE—GAP MODEL: SERVICES

Instructions: List all of the steps involved in a service procedure for the institution, any relevant vendors, and the guests within the seven categories listed below. Incorporate comments and feedback from staff, vendors, and guests about the efficacy of each category. Determine whether any or all of the five potential GAPs are occurring.

Completion Time: one to three hours

Issue:

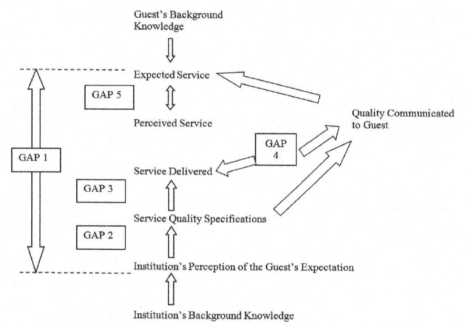

Figure 11.7. GAP model: Services.

GAP 1—the processes from Expected Service through Institution's Perception of Guest's Expectation

GAP 2—the process between the Institution's Perception of the Guest's Expectation to Service Quality Specifications

GAP 3—the process between Service Quality Specifications and the Service Delivered

GAP 4—the difference between the Service Delivered and the Quality Communicated to the Guest

GAP 5—the difference between the Expected Service and the Perceived Service

MODEL TWO: RISK MITIGATION MODEL

Instructions: Write down the project or risk issue that requires mitigation. Summarize each risk. Assess the Severity and Probability as low, medium, or high. List the warning signs for each risk and then develop a mitigation plan for the risk. This exercise may be completed as a group or as individuals and then merged into a group document.

Completion Time: one to three hours

Table 11.13. Risk Mitigation Model

Issue:

Risk	Severity	Probability	Warning Signs	Mitigation Plan

MODEL THREE: PESTLE

Instructions: Describe the issue to be analyzed. Identify the Environmental Factors in each of the six categories. Depending on the issue, you may not be able to identify factors in all of the categories, or you may identify multiple factors in one or several categories. Determine the Current and Future Impacts of those factors on your institution. Develop responses to those Current and Future Impacts. This exercise may be completed as a group or as individuals and then merged into a group document.

Completion Time: one to six hours

Table 11.14. PESTLE Model

Issue:

Environmental Factor Category	Specific Environmental Factor	Current Impact	Current Response	Future Impact	Future Response
Political					
Economic					
Social					
Technological					
Legal					
Ecological					

MODEL FOUR: SCENARIO PLANNING MATRIX

Instructions: This ten-step process is probably best completed in two stages. First, define the scope and time frame for the strategy that requires the generation of these scenarios. Determine the starting point. Then identify the variables and the potential outcomes derived from those variables. You may want to use a PESTLE analysis to uncover potential variables and outcomes. Completing these first four steps can be time intensive. Pausing after completing these steps is highly recommended. Then rank your variables and select the two most important variables and their accompanying outcomes for the Matrix. Identify each of the four Scenarios and write the detailed stories to explain how the Scenarios will play out. After assigning probabilities to each scenario, craft strategies for how your institution will respond to each scenario. This exercise may be completed as a group or as individuals and then merged into a group document.

Completion Time: five to twenty hours

Scenario Planning Matrix

Subject:
Define the planning scope and time frame:
Determine the starting point:
Identify as many potential variables and outcomes as possible:
Rank the variables:
Select the two most important variables and complete the table:

Table 11.15. Scenario Planning Matrix

		Variable 1:	
		Outcome 1a:	**Outcome 1b:**
Variable 2:	**Outcome 2a:**	**Scenario 1:**	**Scenario 2:**
	Outcome 2b:	**Scenario 3:**	**Scenario 4:**

Write detailed scenarios to describe how you expect the scenario to unfold:
Assess the likelihood of each scenario:
Create strategies to manage each scenario:

RESOURCE LIST

ANALYTICAL TOOL BOOK

Brassard, Michael, and Diane Ritter. *The Memory Jogger II*. Methuen, MA: GOAL/QPC, 1994.

MUSEUM MANAGEMENT PUBLICATIONS

Manual of Museum Planning: Sustainable Space, Facilities, and Operations. Edited by Barry Lord, Gail Dexter Lord, and Lindsay Martin. 3rd ed. Lanham, MD: AltaMira Press, 2012.
Small Museum Toolkit. Edited by Cinnamon Catlin-Legutko and Stacy Klingler. Lanham, MD: AltaMira Press, 2012.

PROFESSIONAL ASSOCIATIONS—MUSEUM

American Alliance of Museums. http://www.aam-us.org
American Association for State and Local History. http://www.aaslh.org
National Council on Public History. http://www.ncph.org

PROFESSIONAL ASSOCIATIONS AND CLASSES— PROJECT MANAGEMENT

American Association for State and Local History Continuing Education Series. http://learn .aaslh.org
Center for Nonprofit Management. http://www.cnm.org
International Project Management Association. http://www.ipma.world
Project Management Institute. https://www.pmi.org
Project Management Institute Educational Foundation. http://www.pmief.org

PROJECT MANAGEMENT TOOLS

Asana Project Management Tools. https://asana.com
Basecamp Online Workspace. https://basecamp.com
dapulse Project Management Tool. http://www.dapulse.com
QuickBase Productivity Apps. http://www.quickbase.com
Taskworld. http://www.taskworld.com
Trello Project Management Software. https://trello.com

REPORT AND VISUALIZATION TOOLS

easel.ly Infographics. http://www.easel.ly
infogr.am Charts and Infographics. http://www.infogr.am
Omeka Web Publishing Software. https://omeka.org
Piktochart Easy to Use Infographic Maker. http://www.piktochart.com
Prezi Presentation Software. https://prezi.com

RESEARCH RESOURCES

American Association for State and Local History Visitors Count!—Visitor Research Program. http://tools.aaslh.org/visitors-count/
Center for the Future of Museums. "Trendswatch." http://www.aam-us.org/resources/center-for-the-future-of-museums/projects-and-reports/trendswatch
Dun and Bradstreet Credit and Risk Products. http://www.dnb.com/products/finance-credit-risk.html
Guidestar Nonprofit Reports and Form 990s. http://www.guidestar.org
Institute of Museum and Library Services Data Collection. https://www.imls.gov/research-tools/data-collection
International Council of Museums Information Centre. http://icom.museum/resources/unesco-icom-museum-information-centre/
MarketResearch.com. http://www.marketresearch.com
Pew Research Center: Polling and Demographic Research. http://www.pewresearch.org
United States Census Bureau Data. http://www.census.gov/data/data-tools.html
World Bank Countries and Economies Data. http://data.worldbank.org/country

INDEX

ABOUT THE AUTHOR

Samantha Chmelik is a public historian at Preston Argus, LLC. She has worked and volunteered at libraries, museums, and nonprofit organizations for two decades, developing areas of expertise in research, project management, strategic planning, and best practices/benchmarking. She is the author of *Museum and Historic Site Management: A Case Study Approach*. After receiving a BA from Wellesley College, Chmelik then earned an MS in library and information science from Simmons GSLIS, an MBA from the University of Illinois–Chicago, and an MA in public history from Loyola University, Chicago.

CPSIA information can be obtained
at www.ICGtesting.com
Printed in the USA
BVOW04*1625120217
475904BV00006B/8/P

9 781442 270473